out of bounds

Studies in the
Postmodern Theory of Education

Joe L. Kincheloe and Shirley R. Steinberg
General Editors

Vol. 363

PETER LANG
New York • Washington, D.C./Baltimore • Bern
Frankfurt am Main • Berlin • Brussels • Vienna • Oxford

JABARI MAHIRI & DEREK VAN RHEENEN

out of bounds

WHEN SCHOLARSHIP ATHLETES
BECOME ACADEMIC SCHOLARS

PETER LANG
New York • Washington, D.C./Baltimore • Bern
Frankfurt am Main • Berlin • Brussels • Vienna • Oxford

Library of Congress Cataloging-in-Publication Data

Mahiri, Jabari.
Out of bounds: when scholarship athletes become academic scholars /
Jabari Mahiri, Derek Van Rheenen.
p. cm. — (Counterpoints: studies in the
postmodern theory of education; v. 363)
Includes bibliographical references.
1. College sports—United States.
2. College athletes—Education—United States.
3. Education, Higher—Aims and objectives—United States.
I. Van Rheenen, Derek. II. Title.
GV351.M34   796.04'30973—dc22   2009045809
ISBN 978-1-4331-0569-2 (hardcover)
ISBN 978-1-4331-0568-5 (paperback)
ISSN 1058-1634

Bibliographic information published by **Die Deutsche Nationalbibliothek**.
Die Deutsche Nationalbibliothek lists this publication in the "Deutsche
Nationalbibliografie"; detailed bibliographic data is available
on the Internet at http://dnb.d-nb.de/.

The paper in this book meets the guidelines for permanence and durability
of the Committee on Production Guidelines for Book Longevity
of the Council of Library Resources.

© 2010 Peter Lang Publishing, Inc., New York
29 Broadway, 18th floor, New York, NY 10006
www.peterlang.com

Printed in the United States of America

To Herbert D. Simons

Pioneer of Athletic and Academic Achievement

CONTENTS

ACKNOWLEDGMENTS

Mojgan Jelveh is the unsung hero of the *Out of Bounds* group. She graciously helped the group document its efforts and clarify its direction. This book would not have been possible without her contributions. We thank the six informants, Erin Conner Ngeno, Anne Gregory, Malo Hutson, Ernest Morrell, Anthony Smith, and Derek Van Rheenen, who allowed us to tell their stories in order to illuminate and implicate ways that sport and schooling may be better understood and constructively changed. Others also played key roles in the *Out of Bounds* group that we acknowledge and thank: Steven Doten, Jeff Duncan Andrade, Andy Gonzalez, and Clarence Phelps. We thank Rick Ayers for bringing fresh eyes to a reading of this work, and also Billie Jo Conlee and Rosa Garcia for their generous help in so many ways. We also thank our Series Editors, Shirley R. Steinberg and Joe L. Kincheloe, as well as Peter Lang's Managing Director Christopher Myers and Production Editor Bernadette Shade. Additionally, we thank Colin Lankshear and Michele Knobel for providing early support and insightful responses to this work. Finally, we acknowledge the importance of the collaborative process that produced this work and its value for our roles as co-authors.

The research for this book was supported by a grant from the University of California, Committee on Research.

· 1 ·

DESIRE AND DISDAIN

In the U.S. as in other societies, athletes and sport signify complex, variegated meanings and emotions that range from desire to disdain. Wideman suggested, "Our current popular culture would be incomprehensible to an outsider unless he or she understood basketball as the key to deciphering speech styles, clothing styles, and metaphors employed by kids, politicians, and housewives" (1992: 151). An extension of this point can be seen in the story about Craig Robinson, who became the head coach of men's basketball at Oregon State, being asked by his younger sister Michele to vet a suitor named Barack Obama by assessing his character via the litmus test of a pickup basketball game. As a former student in the Chicago Public Schools, Robinson has his own amazing story that links an eventual Ivy League education and prowess in sport to the idealized promise of America. He sized up the law school grad as someone who could shoot and create, shared the ball, yet as a lefty tended to favor playing to that side of the court. In the end he gave his approval, and, of course, it was based on much more than how Barack Obama played basketball.

The pervasiveness of sport in our lives and imaginations is spearheaded by athletic icons that inspire us to "be like Mike," or more currently Tiger and LeBron. Dyson's (1993) critique of this phenomenon is also apropos for the new "Mikes" of today. He contended that the "cultural canonization of Michael Jordan provokes reflection about the contradictory uses to which Jordan's body is put as a seminal cultural text and ambiguous symbol of fantasy, and the avenues of agency and resistance available especially to black youth who make symbolic investments in Jordan's body as a means of cultural and personal possibility, creativity and desire" (64–65). The athletic body as a cultural text is also subjected to particular kinds of readings in the context of schools, readings that invoke coded and often contradictory conceptions of mental and physical divides, of masculinity and femininity, of pleasure and pain, of agency and identity, of race and social class. The key question for the research presented in this book was what were the constraints and possibilities of athletes moving beyond boundaries and trajectories of sporting practices to become professional scholars, and what do these understandings suggest for how sport and school experiences for young people can be made to better support their intellectual and physical growth and development. The key method was to collaboratively generate, document, and analyze life stories from the cases of six informants, men and women who were highly successful scholarship athletes but went on to become prolific academic scholars.

Findings from this critical, participatory, qualitative research (Brodley, 1987) challenge prevalent perceptions limiting the dialectic of athletics and academics. They do so by providing insights into the nature and motives of educational and societal structures and practices (embodied in both institutions and individuals) that perpetuate notions of mental/physical divides and essentialize and denigrate diverse bodily experiences while elevating a separated life of the mind. The findings specifically reveal how academic and intellectual space for scholarship athletes as potential scholars is often demarcated and confined in subtle and overt ways connected to perceptions of race, gender, and sexual orientation along with perceptions of physical and intellectual capabilities, and how all this is ingrained and sustained in the social geography of educational institutions. In the concluding chapter, we connect findings derived from the detailed discussion of the experiences of our six informants that are revealed in chapters two, three, and four to a number of significant implications for transforming practices in and between sport and school.

Bogdan and Biklen (1992) noted that researchers doing certain kinds of case studies usually fall into them: "They do not decide on the 'type' of subject they want to interview and then go out looking for an example. Rather, they meet a person who strikes them as a good subject and then decide to pursue it" (65). This is what happened with our six informants whose intricate and interwoven life stories, dialogues, interviews, writings, personal artifacts, and critical reflections provided the substance for this book.

The analysis and presentation of this qualitative data have been constructed as "narratives of intentionality" that reveal how the lives of these informants challenged institutionalized divisions of sport and artificial distinctions between the body and mind. These narratives of their performative efforts to navigate the classroom and the playing field provided searing insights into how, why, and in whose interest particular lines of demarcation are drawn. Their individual experiences offered multiple lenses through which to view the intersecting spaces of sport, schooling, and society as complex systems consisting of organizations, institutions, and individuals interacting, adapting, and potentially changing.

Significantly, the character of these changes often corresponded to ways that individuals operated as actors or agents. We began to better understand how the court, the track, and the playing field had been socially constructed and bounded as specific kinds of spaces—de-realized and specular, governed by rules and rituals, and predicated on performance. The informants had initially been actors (directed and scripted performers) who eventually struggled to become agents who took responsibility for the direction of their lives. They were supported in this struggle by significant others and critical events in their social contexts. Becoming agentive connected to each informant's development of a somatic awareness, a kinesthetic consciousness in understanding how the body is racialized, gendered, and commodified in sport, education, and society.

Anthony (Tony) Smith, Derek Van Rheenen, Ernest Morrell, Malo Hutson, Anne Gregory, and Erin Conner Ngeno were not only informants, however. In unique ways they also acted as principal collaborators in the research and writing of this work. Tony, Derek, and Anne are white, and Ernest, Malo, and Erin are black. We know that these racial designations are socially constructed as ranked categories that were developed following, and in conjunction with, global expansions of power and domination by western Europeans starting in the 1400s. Essentially, race is not real as a meaningful biological construct. There is no real line in nature between one racial category and another. Yet, as a systematized hierarchy of difference ingrained in social relations, race is experienced as a daily reality. So, we have acknowledged categories of race along with social class and gender in order to further problematize them through the insights of our informants from their experiences in sport and school. Their individual stories; their distinct personal, racial, and gendered identities; their varying class and cultural backgrounds; and their different sporting and learning experiences were not as significant in isolation, however, as they were when integrated and made to interact to generate what we call "dialogic data."

We define dialogic data as documented group engagements in dialogues

directed toward generating, illuminating, and complicating meanings of assemblages of narrative, interview, and reflective texts along with other material artifacts connected to a set of life experiences that the group members have in
common. The common thread was that focal informants were all gifted scholarship athletes who eventually became highly successful academic scholars.
Analysis and interpretation of this dialogic data were central components of a
systematic process for apprehending the provocative patterns, conflicts, and
themes that permeated their stories, and this process uniquely revealed something of the complexity of how these individuals were dynamically engaged in
sport and school.

Tony, Derek, Ernest and Malo were all in graduate school at the University
of California, Berkeley (also known as "Cal" or "Berkeley") a little more than
a decade ago. During that time in 1997, Derek was just completing his doctorate in Cultural Studies; Tony and Ernest were working on their doctorates in
Education; and Malo was completing a Master's Degree in City and Regional
Planning. These four men and three others—Jeff Duncan Andrade, Andy
Gonzalez, and Clarence Phelps (exceptional athletes who were also Berkeley
graduate students in education at that time)—began a series of group dialogues to unpack the nature of their intersecting experiences of athletics and
academics. The meetings for these discussions were initiated and coordinated
by Jabari Mahiri and Mojgan Jelveh, the former a Berkeley Professor of
Education and the latter a Berkeley doctoral student in education.

Jeff, Andy, and Clarence made key contributions to the initial series of dialogues, interviews, and personal reflections in this project. Jeff was a dominant
soccer and basketball player in high school and college. He completed his
doctorate in 2002 and became a professor of education at San Francisco State
University. Andy played football at Cal for four years and then became an assistant coach for the team while going to graduate school. After running track as
an undergraduate at Cal, Clarence continued his athletic career while in graduate school, and at the time of our initial meetings, he had placed 6th in the
nationals in track competition. For various reasons, however, these three men
decided not to be focal informants for this book. Later, we connected with Anne
in School Psychology and Erin in the Graduate School of Education who
became interested in the project while working on their doctorates at Berkeley.
They had experienced their own versions of the intersecting dynamics of athletics and academics as women, and with their consent to become informants,
we all felt that significant contributions would be made to this work through
presenting their stories in conjunction with those of the men. Consequently,
Erin and Anne joined Tony, Derek, Ernest, and Malo as our six primary

collaborator/informants.

Initially, the design of the project was for each participant to be a co-author in the writing of this book. Jabari and Derek developed a rhizomatic strategy for writing the individual stories that designated teams of two that were responsible for writing on the lives of specific participants with each writing duo utilizing all our accumulated sources of data. These collaborative write-ups were to be responded to and revised in subsequent sessions by the whole group of participants. However, the intensity of graduate studies made it difficult for the group to complete this aspect of the work, and things became dormant for quite a while. Yet, most of the participants strongly felt that these provocative stories needed to be told. Eventually, Jabari and Derek were "authorized" through the consent and support of Tony, Malo, Ernest, Erin, and Anne to complete the documentation and write up the descriptions of how members of the group had stepped outside of the bounded roles and trajectories of scholarship athletes to become highly successful scholars in and beyond the academy.

One benefit in this work *not* being published earlier is that the lives and professional careers of these men and women have now been more fully revealed. Mostly, what could have been said when this project was initiated was that each participant was a promising young scholar in a very competitive program at a highly selective university. Now, their substantial scholarly and professional achievements are clearly evident. For example, each participant except Malo went on to complete a doctorate at the University of California, Berkeley. Malo finished a Masters degree at Berkeley and then completed a doctorate at the Massachusetts Institute of Technology.

The academic careers of these men and women have been prolific. For example, on May 21, 2009 after working at the highest levels in San Francisco and Emeryville California school districts, Tony (who finished his Ph.D. in 2002) was unanimously selected by the seven-member school board to be the new Superintendent of Oakland Public Schools. As an athlete Tony had been captain of Cal's football team and later played professionally for the Green Bay Packers and the San Francisco 49ers. Derek played professional soccer for a number of years for the San Francisco Bay Blackhawks after he graduated from Cal as an Academic All-American. He received his Ph.D. in 1997 and has worked as the Director of the Athletic Study Center as well as the Director and a professor in the graduate program on Cutural Studies of Sport in Education at Berkeley. In 2008 he was inducted into Cal's Athletic Hall of Fame.

Ernest and Malo did not go pro after college though both clearly had that potential. Ernest had been a basketball and track star in high school, and he was on a full track scholarship while he completed a degree in English at UC

Santa Barbara. Instead of aspiring to a professional career in sport, he went to graduate school and completed a Ph.D. in 2001. Like Derek a few years earlier, he won the school's outstanding dissertation award; was also awarded a prestigious two-year Post-Doctoral Fellowship by the American Educational Research Association; had multiple offers for tenure-track positions at research universities; has published five well received academic books between 2004 and 2009 [almost a book a year during this period]; and Ernest is now a tenured, Associate Professor of Education at UCLA. Malo's primary sport in high school and college was baseball. He was scouted as a prospect by the Toronto Blue Jays while he was still in high school but decided to go to college instead. He played baseball for Cal, but for reasons we discuss later, he quit the team after his junior year despite again being a prime prospect to be a professional baseball player. He completed his Ph.D. in 2006 and, similar to Ernest, had multiple, impressive academic job offers while simultaneously being awarded a prestigious Post-Doctoral Fellowship as a Robert Wood Johnson Foundation Health and Society Scholar in the Department of Epidemiology at the University of Michigan. In 2008 he selected Berkeley over several other offers as the university to begin as an Assistant Professor in its Department of City and Regional Planning.

Anne and Erin didn't have significant opportunities to become professionals in their sports because of the dearth or absence of professional women's teams, but both had major athletic achievements. Anne played softball, basketball, and soccer on division winning teams in high school, and in soccer she played on the boy's team for three years as the only female in the school's entire soccer league. Similar to Derek, Anne received the scholar/athlete award from her school. She also played Division I women's soccer as an undergraduate at Brown. She completed a Ph.D. in 2005 in Clinical and Community Psychology at Berkeley, became a licensed Clinical Psychologist, and received multiple offers at research universities before selecting the University of Virginia to begin as an Assistant Professor in its Clinical and School Psychology program. She was awarded the Outstanding Doctoral Dissertation Award for Division K of the American Educational Research Association. Erin's undergraduate degree at Berkeley was in integrative biology. However, she went into education for a Master's degree, and completed a Ph.D. in education in 2007. Soon afterwards, she was awarded a highly competitive Post-Doctoral Fellowship in Berkeley's Biology Scholars Program. Before transferring to complete her undergraduate studies at Cal, Erin played basketball in high school and at Oakwood College in Alabama. Like Anne in soccer, Erin had many experiences playing basketball with men as the sole woman in the game.

The Narrative Turn

Postmodern sensibilities in part reflect experiments with composing ethnographies in new ways, including the emergence of a "narrative turn" and appreciation for storytelling as a source of unique insights into cultural practices (Denzin and Lincoln, 2003). Simply put, storytelling is a meaning making process, a way of knowing. Vygotsky (1987) noted, "Every word that people use in telling their stories is a microcosm of their consciousness" (236–237). Because people engage social issues and institutions through concrete experiences, their stories as ways of knowing provide multiple understandings of the nature of social structures and processes.

The collaborative generation, documentation, and analysis of our informants' life stories were framed by the notion that there is no one reality. Rather, reality and meaning lie in ways that individuals' experiences ultimately re-shape their reality (Riessman, 1993: 16). This approach is also grounded in beliefs that the self (and thus identity) is socially constructed (Casey, 1995: 222; Laslett & Thorne, 1997: 6), multi-faceted, and complex (Ferdman, 1990). It recognizes that relations of power are continually at work, that objective structures exist "independent of the consciousness and desires of agents and are capable of guiding or constraining their practices or their representations" (Bourdieu, 1990:123), but that active, individual choices can also work against these constraints. Consequently, we saw the participant's stories both as "a means by which identities may be fashioned" (Rosenwald and Ochberg, 1992) as well as a means by which culture is expressed (Riessman, 1993). Riessman further noted that "respondents narrativize particular experiences in their lives often where there has been a breach between ideal and real, self and society" (3). In a variety of ways, each of our informants had come to see a breach between their sense of themselves as becoming scholars and ways that school and society worked to constrain them as athletes only.

So the stories of our informants, in part, are stories of becoming—stories of what these six individuals have become despite conflicting institutional intentions. In this process of becoming, we found that there was an intentional turn of events, as these individuals began to see themselves as scholars, educators and social agents of change. The narrative turn, as articulated in their own story-telling of themselves as scholars, was qualitatively different for each of these individuals. Their movement in a similar direction was likewise limited by structures of power, privilege and possibility. The different meanings constructed around this educational mobility, a social and somatic consciousness of turning, depended on the unique set of social positions or circumstances experienced by the six informants. The original group of participants tried to work in a novel way to generate and interpret the textual materials that enabled the writing of these stories. This work began with a series of meetings in which the participants engaged in extended discussions of a wide range of sporting and schooling experiences that brought them to that time in their lives when they were all in graduate school. Mojgan Jelveh was the only woman participant at that time, and her background was not that of an athlete. Rather, her participation was based on a keen personal interest in the focus and process of these discussions, and without her contributions [noted in the Acknowledgments] this book would not have been possible.

A central feature and product of this process was the creation of the dialogic data. There were ten meetings for discussions of the group over the course of 18 months, and each one lasted for approximately three hours. Seven of these meetings were taperecorded and transcribed, and the text was made available to participants prior to the following meeting so that earlier issues and themes could be reviewed and discussed more fully in subsequent meetings. Part of the first meeting was used to collectively construct questions for a demographic profile that each participant completed to provide consistent information on family, cultural, socio-economic, and educational backgrounds. We also collaborated on a set of 25 interview questions that each participant later wrote individual responses to. The questions were designed as prompts to get participants to think freely and expansively about their experiences. We decided that each participant would also write extended personal reflections of his experiences in sport and school as well as share material artifacts like newspaper articles, award announcements, video clips, recruitment letters, and school transcripts that provided additional documentation of their athletic and academic performances.

Erin and Anne were not at these meetings, but they eventually wrote to the exact demographic, interview, and personal reflection prompts that the earlier participants had written to, and they also provided key artifacts connected to their lives in sport and school. The empirical materials from everyone were copied and shared with all of our participants, and these increasingly rich assemblages became the corpus of materials that focused and motivated continuing dialogues and the eventual writing of this book.

Rather than the analysis and interpretations of these data being made by a unitary researcher, this work ultimately leveraged the multiplicity of perspectives that were distributed throughout the group of participants. The analysis was continually sharpened and extended through critique in the dialogic exchanges. Our work toward consensus on the meanings of the myriad facts and reflections captured in the data allowed us to both separate and blend multiple perspectives in the representation of individual selves refracted through the prism of others. As we created this process Tony commented, "This is really exciting because there is so much overlay, so many boundary crossings. We have athletes who became scholars who are writing responses to the stories of other athletes who became scholars. Then we have everyone's different perspectives on the same individual, and so on." This dialogic approach to capturing and interpreting the varied personal experiences, the introspections, the responses to interview questions, and the presentation of material artifacts in order to narrate the moments and meanings of sport and schooling in these individuals' lives gave this work a rhizomatic quality in its attempt to approach understandings through multiple entryways (Deleuze and Guattari, 1987). This valuing of the multiple, the attempt to make a rhizome system, was a principle enacted to disrupt the privileging of hierarchical systems of meaning making and transmission through the construction of collaborative narratives.

The following dialogue from one of the meetings in 1997 exemplifies how this collaborative process yielded insights into identities, including academic identities, as they were being forged in sporting practices. We had each read and written responses to Tony's personal statement. These written responses were read out loud and then there was further discussion by the group on the evolving issues. Tony's statement had, in part, discussed his budding relationship with the poet Emily Dickinson at a time when his mom had left him and moved to Los Angeles while he was in fifth grade. He revealed how he had come to see sport as a way out of the poverty of his childhood. "It was like, play football and get out, or go in the army, or stay there and go to jail, pretty much." So, he felt lucky to eventually get a scholarship to a Division I university. "I feel I was brought in [to Cal] to do a job," he had written. "Win football games. I sacrificed my body for life for the sport I loved."

Malo's written response noted that Tony's description of the commodification of his body also seemed related to Ernest's personal statement that had been discussed in an earlier meeting which equated how he had been treated in sport to slave labor. In the ensuing discussion, Tony responded to this point. "There are so many whitenesses and blacknesses," he told the group. "All these spectrums of being are just burned into my memory....I'll never forget being seven years old when my mom didn't have enough food stamps to pay for the groceries," he continued. "The food stamps in the first place, and then not having enough. We had to pick things to put back, and it was just this little town where everyone knew everyone....Marty and Cindy, my mother and father; they were 15 and 16 when I was born. I don't hold them accountable at all for what happened, because they were kids, right....[But] that leads into the notion of viable alternatives; I didn't have any viable alternatives....My mom moved to L.A., and I lived fifth grade all by myself. I started reading Emily Dickinson then, and I wrote to her....It's hard to talk about this stuff actually. Writing verse in adverse conditions....Literally, that's how it happened."

The irony was noted that eleven years later, Tony wrote his senior thesis on Emily Dickinson for a Bachelor's degree in English at Berkeley. Additional insights emerged as the discussion of his personal statement continued in that meeting.

Jabari: On this Emily Dickinson connection, there is an interesting absence of the mom and presence of this imaginary woman.

Tony: I'd like to say that it was serendipity, but...it was random that I pulled that book out of the library. I used to go to the library in 4th grade. That was my thing. But, yeah, I started reading Emily Dickinson and learned about her, and [it was] a way out....We could talk about her all night.

Ernest: Poem by poem.

Tony: Exactly. Like another Emily Dickinson moment was her poem "Because I Could Not Stop for Death," death stopped for me. It was like, I won't stop....She mirrored this, this woman, her intense fire.

Jabari: In a way your litany of injuries is a kind of replication of "Because I Could Not Stop for Death," so death stopped for me"....You know, the...limitations of the body gave way to the physical demands of the sport.

Ernest: I read Tony's personal statement, and it was heavy. A couple of things came to mind...[like] choosing English as a major for its solitude. But there was something missing from your description of yourself as an athlete. Your body was your capital, but the harder you worked it the more alienated you became from it. So, who better to provide solace than a writer like Emily Dickinson?

Literally, there were two distinct personas. Tony the good football player who plays through injuries, who busts his shoulder, gets it rebuilt and is right back out there....And, then there is Tony the literary scholar who is reading about this person...[who] locks herself in a room and doesn't want to deal with anybody because she recognizes the hypocrisy and a lot of things that people aren't willing to admit.

So, it's natural that the two go together. Someone who is as smart as you, and someone who is as critical as you, but who needs football so much that you can't be critical. So, all that anger, and all that frustration, and all that built up animosity is let out through reading and literature.

In his first two seasons, Tony had to get three major surgeries, two to completely reconstruct each shoulder and one to have a plastic knuckle inserted in his finger after it had been severely broken—injuries that ultimately ended his professional career in football.

Derek, on the other hand, made a personal choice to end his athletic career after playing professional soccer for five years. The message he always received from his family, peers, and neighbors while growing up in the affluent town of Woodside, California, was that professional sports were not a serious career choice—"sport was recreation from the real world." His great grandmother was a poet; his mother was a psychologist; his father was a doctor who also taught at Stanford Medical School; his aunt and uncle were college professors. "When I was drafted to play," Derek wrote, "I always thought of it as a hiatus from real life. Playing professional sports for me was a prolonging of adolescence." However, despite being selected to be an Academic All-American and majoring in political economy with a 3.6 GPA, he reported, "The school didn't make a big deal about it…didn't in fact say a word to me. It was typical of the way that the Athletic Department…[was] out of touch with the academic portion of student athletes' education.…[They were] much more impressed that I went on to play professional soccer than that I went on to earn a Ph.D. and became a professor."

The stories of Ernest, Malo, Erin and Anne were also complicated and conflicted. They illuminate ways that social class, race, gender, and sexuality are put into play in sport and society. The group discussions were occasions for making critical connections to the differing life stories of the informants. When Tony talked about "writing verse in adverse conditions," for example, or about coming to see sport as form of tracking within the processes of schools, these were not his words originally. The former words came from Derek's written response to Tony's personal reflection, and the latter idea was put forth initially by another participant to which Tony added a perception of how "living *down* to expectations was something we all went through." A defining feature of this dialogic process was the way it allowed the participants to continually put new ideas into each other's heads that led to richer understandings of everyone's experiences. It allowed us to both separate and synthesize the various ways that participants had attempted to understand the tightly bounded and coded identities they had been "coached" to accept on playing fields and "taught" to accept in school. In both arenas, the body was disciplined and trained to be a "good" student and "good" athlete.

Conceptual Frames

We have mentioned the rhizome, and in its articulation by Deleuze and Guattari (1987) the image of the tree as a system and philosophy of hierarchical organization of ideas, institutions, individuals, etc, is supplanted by an image of a subterranean stem, or bulb. They show that "the Tree or Root as an image, endlessly develops the law of the One that becomes two, then of the two that become four….Binary logic is the spiritual reality of the root-tree" (5). The tree image that has been pervasively used to organize Western imagination is rooted in reproduction of simple dualisms. Deleuze and Guattari contrasted this orientational frame to that of a multiplicity of access points and connectivities in a rhizomatic system like underground bulbs or tubers. They noted that two of the key principles of this system are "connection and heterogeneity: any point of a rhizome can be connected to any other, and must be. This is very different from the tree or root, which plots a point, fixes an order" (7). We attempted a rhizomatic approach to the assemblages and interpretations of our data in order to honor and access multiple points of entry, novel connectivities, and a democracy of ideas in telling the informants' stories of individual but overlapping struggles to step outside socially constructed boundaries of sport and into new arenas of awareness and identifications as scholars.

In addition to the rhizome, we used several other conceptual frames to focus and refine our depictions and discussions in this book. Bourdieu's (1990; 1992) notions of fields in the space of sporting practices; Bakhtin's (1981) notion of chronotopes; Willis' (1990) notions of a grounded aesthetics; Pratt's (1992) notion of contact zones; Giroux's (1994) notion of border identities; and Gilroy (1993) and Carter's (1992) notions of movement as a mode of being were joined with work from a number of discourse theorists and the methods for analyzing life stories to fully interpret and integrate the substance of our informants' lives. These frameworks were studied and discussed by the participants, and they allowed us to better capture the ways that each informant uniquely articulated his or her identity with respect to key patterns, conflicts, themes, and interpersonal relationships that we found across all of the individual narratives.

Bourdieu (1990) set out several key principles that helped frame our thinking about the intersections of sports, schools, and society. First, he suggested "that it is impossible to analyze a particular sport independently of the set of sporting practices," and that "one has to imagine the space of sporting practices as a system from which every element derives its distinctive value" (156). He additionally noted, "This space of sports has first of all to be related to the social space that is expressed in it" (157). He then made the following important connection: "the correspondence, which is a real homology, is established between the space of sporting practices, or more precisely, the space of the different finely analyzed modalities of the practice of different sports, and the space of social positions. It is in the relation between these two spaces that the pertinent properties of every sporting practice are defined" (p. 158).

This perspective that the pertinent properties of sporting practices become meaningful in terms of the social spaces they internally reveal as well as in terms of their place as spaces inside the larger space of societal positions provided an important conceptual bi-focal. It was useful for examining the particular sporting practices of our informants and assessing what they revealed about social positions and positioning inside and outside of their respective sports. Bourdieu (1990) refers to his concept of the field as the social contexts of action within which individuals act. It is of note that Bourdieu also refers to the conceptual notion of the field as a game, with differentiated chances for individuals to win or lose. As Thompson argued in the Introduction to Bourdieu's *Language and Symbolic Power*, "all individuals, whatever their aims and chances of success, will share in common certain fundamental presuppositions. All participants must believe in the game they are playing, and in the value of what is at stake in the struggles they are waging. The very existence and persistence of the game or field presupposes a total and unconditional 'investment,' a practical and unquestioning belief in the game and its stakes. Hence the conduct of struggle within a field, whether a conflict over the distribution of wealth or over the value of a work of art, always presupposes a fundamental accord or complicity on the part of those who participate in the struggle." So, part of our project was to delineate both the structures and meanings of the space of sporting practices as they were experienced by our informants. As researchers, this required that we not merely draw the shapes, but also uncover and depict the dynamic interrelationships of these complex spaces.

Bourdieu (1990) noted the importance of focusing on inter-relationships by calling attention to the fact that the "space of sports is not a universe closed in on itself. It is inserted into a universe of practices and consumptions themselves structured and constituted as a system" (159). He cautioned researchers to not forget "that this space is the locus of forces which do not apply only to it" (159). Through our detailed examinations of the experiences of our six informants (examinations of definitive sub-spaces that they inhabited) we endeavored as Bourdieu suggested "to construct a summary description of the whole of the space considered" (160).

To augment our focus on the space of sports in society, we turned to Bakhtin's notion of the chronotope. Bakhtin (1981) formulated the chronotope as "a unit of analysis for studying texts according to the ratio and the nature of the temporal and spatial categories represented" (426). Although he was discussing the reading of texts, we felt the concept of the chronotope was also viable as a way of reading sport and the embodied athlete as a dynamic text in the dominant narratives of U.S. society. Consistent with how Bakhtin suggested that "the chronotope is an optic for reading texts as x-rays of the forces at work in the culture system from which they spring" (426), we saw how our reading of the space of sport was an optic for seeing the working of societal forces. Like Dyson's textual reading of Michael Jordan, we found that sport replicated or uniquely illuminated some of the temporal and spatial categories of the dominant society. In other words, our reading of the embedded relationships of sport in society through the lenses of the experiences of our six informants grounded a partial reading of larger forces at work in the culture.

Following Bakhtin, Gilroy (1993) used the ship as a novel chronotope "to rethink modernity via the history of the black Atlantic and the African Diaspora into the western hemisphere" (17). He "emphasised that ships were the living means by which the points within that Atlantic world were joined. They were mobile elements that stood for the shifting spaces in between the fixed places that they connected" (16). In a similar way, we saw the space of sport (the court, the track, the playing field) as both embedded within and shifting between societal spaces (its structures, meanings, and forces) in such an integral way that the former could be seen as multiple x-rays of the latter. As we worked inside the space of sports, we realized that we could not simply understand it as a metaphor or microcosm of the workings of other structures in society, and that this was not Gilroy's intent with a chronotopical framing. In using this framing for the dynamics of sport, we saw that much more was involved than replicating dynamics of the larger society on a smaller scale. There are ways, of course, that sport practices mirror larger social practices, yet our priority was to capture the definitive character of sporting practices as they are imbedded in, yet in dynamic interaction with, society. In meticulously working out the particular spaces of sport in detail, we began to better understand the nature of its fluid and intricate engagements with society and schools. Like Gilroy's ship, we saw the space of sport having qualities of stasis and motion as it moves in between other cultural institutions while having a culture of its own.

Willis (1990) was useful in facilitating our understanding of the functional and symbolic character of sport practices. He invested much of his theoretical formulations of a dynamic, common culture into the notion of a grounded aesthetics. He wrote, "grounded aesthetics are the specifically creative and dynamic moments of a whole process of cultural life, of cultural birth and rebirth" (22). This notion of grounded aesthetics highlights the active agency of cultural consumers, producing symbolic action and creativity in their daily practices. For our purposes we tried to connect Willis' focus on the active body as a symbolic resource, particularly as individuals and groups negotiate social meaning through games and sports. He noted, for example, "sports and games provide materials, activities and social relationships which have symbolic as well as physical meanings and uses. They provide resources towards the symbolic work of cultural expression and formation of cultural identity" (109). What he revealed in his discussion of sport as a symbolic resource was the sociability of an embodied practice, the ability of individuals to creatively articulate identity in relationship to others through shared practices.

The works of several other scholars were also useful for comprehending the dynamic interactions and intersections of the space of sports. For example, though Pratt (1992) proposes the concept of "contact zone" to describe the creative aspects of colonial cultural encounters, there were interesting ways that this concept was also applicable to sport. In addition to issues of domination and subjugation, contact zones revealed the intricate ways in which new identities and new cultural categories were being continually negotiated between dominant and subjugated groups. Roediger (1991), Aronowitz and Giroux (1991), and others have shown how it is not simply whites in the dominant groups and people of color in the subjugated ones, but that increasingly, working-class whites are also realizing themselves to be in positions of subjugation. Giroux (1994) echoed the changeability of identities and cultural categories that occurs through the contact of different cultural groups and perspectives. He called for a "need to construct a notion of border identity that challenges any essentialized notion of subjectivity while simultaneously demonstrating that the self as a historical and cultural formation is shaped in complex, related, and multiple ways through its interaction with numerous and diverse communities" (p. 38). In effect our informants created border identities at the intersection of sport and school.

Carter (1992) further deconstructed the notion that the only manifestation of contact between diverse communities, even dominant and subjugated communities, was opposition. He noted, "the opposition between here and there is itself a cultural construction, a consequence of thinking in terms of fixed entities and defining them oppositionally" (101). In images quite consistent with Gilroy's chronotope of ships, Carter went on to suggest that movement between different cultural entities or groups might be seen as more than just an "awkward interval between fixed points of departure and arrival, but as a mode of being in the world. The question would be, then, not how to arrive, but how to move, how to identify convergent and divergent movements" (101). These works by Gilroy, Willis, Pratt, Giroux, and Carter provided viable concepts for exploring the nature and meanings of individual and group movements within and between the space of sport and other social and institution-al spaces in schools and society.

One other avenue into these spaces was in the assessment of attending dis-course practices. Informed by Gee (1990), we explored how discourses of both sport and school (as well as other social spaces) were themselves "ways of behaving, interacting, valuing, thinking, believing, speaking, and often read-ing and writing that are accepted as instantiations of particular roles of specif-ic groups of people" (xix). Fairclough (1992) was useful also in exploring how discourse practices in sport and school could represent acts of agency on the parts of the people involved. He noted, "Firstly, it implies that discourse is a mode of action, one form in which people may act upon the world and espe-cially upon each other, as well as a mode of representation....Secondly, it implies that there is a dialectical relationship between discourse and social struc-ture . . ." (63–64). This helped us focus on the implications of discourses them-selves as forms of social practice, and the fact that people themselves operate in multiple social spaces, some of which may be in conflict with each other. Importantly, these conflicts are both represented and negotiated in discourse practices. The student-athlete negotiates and embodies a complex identity. It is the institutional demarcation of a fixed identity, binary and oppositional in nature, which limits fuller understanding of the nature and possibilities of their experiences of life in and beyond schools.

The formulations of grounded aesthetics, contact zones, border identities, and movement as a mode of being, conjoined with considerations of how each is powerfully mediated in discourse returned us to Bourdieu (1990) and an argu-ment central to this book. He noted that "the same object being supplied could be appropriated by agents endowed with very diverse dispositions" (p. 164). Simply put, *Out of Bounds* is the conscious act of athletes becoming agents in appropriating a synthesis between their bodies and minds in multiple social worlds, and particularly within the academy. One of its main distinctions and strengths is how it gives an in-depth analysis across time; across race, class and gender; and across different sports and sporting practices. In focusing on its informants as active agents and not just passive subjects, *Out of Bounds* goes beyond the limits and contradictions that characterizes much of the work on these issues and offers new ways of thinking about connections between sport and schools.

Summary

The following four chapters amplify the considerations of sport and schooling discussed in this introduction. Chapters two, three, and four depict and critique the life stories focused on the sport and school experiences of our six informants. These chapters are organized as a sequence of class/race/gender duets. Essentially, the dialogic engagement of the three pairs of informants is initiated and sustained chapter by chapter through these middle passages of the book. Chapter two presents the stories of Tony and Derek who are white men; chapter three presents the stories of Ernest and Malo who are black men; and chapter four presents the stories of two women, Anne who is white and Erin who is black. Although organized on the surface into class, race, and gender categories, one of the purposes of these three chapters is to show how these very categories are problematic and overlapping.

Thus, these duets are not so much voices in harmony around class, race, and gender identities or categories. Instead, they are distinct voices in dialogue and critique of their separate paths through sport to becoming academic scholars. The lived experiences of these six individuals, the narrative twists and turns of their stories, blur the boundaries of inclusion and exclusion, privilege and marginalization. The blurring of boundaries likewise challenges the stability and coherence of social categories and divisions, reproduced in the institutional structures of school and sport. The concluding chapter provides a synthesis and analysis that reflects on the stories presented in chapters two, three, and four, again with respect to the conceptual frames and methodology used to generate and explicate these stories. This chapter goes further in linking the separate stories, the distinct gender and racial identities, the varying class and cultural backgrounds, and the different sporting and learning experiences and indicates how they have interacted to yield the key findings of this book. These findings provide a potent challenge to prevalent perceptions of a necessary divide between athletics and academics by identifying and explaining the workings of sports, educational, and societal structures and practices as they are played out in the lives of individuals—practices that subjugate and denigrate bodily experiences in the service of beliefs about the superiority of the mind, and of school over sport rather than a nuanced integration of these social institutions and lived experiences. The final chapter connects our findings to a number of important implications for making the institutions and practices of sport and education more supportive and expansive experience for developing young people's intellectual and physical capabilities in school and life.

Sport in School and Society

We conclude this introductory chapter with a discussion of works that address and attempt to contextualize the space of sport in educational and other societal institutions. As these institutions reflect the cultural values of larger

American society, so too do the varied meanings of sport in society enter the social geography of schools, not only on its athletic fields but also in its class-rooms. Thus, the space of sports, given its historical place within schools, must be further analyzed. Much of the literature related to the focus of this book has focused on the North American phenomenon of intercollegiate athletics and the controversial presence or place of commercialized sports within institutions of higher learning. Backgrounded in the debate over whether varsity sport pro-grams debase the academic ideals of a quality education have been the athletes themselves, the practitioners. When athletes have been featured in the liter-ature, they have tended to be presented as passive subjects of a powerful infra-structure. They are presented as commodified, alienated, exploited (Bacon, 1997; Rigauer, 1981; Eitzen, 2000; Byers and Hammer, 1995; Zimbalist, 2001; Edwards, 1973; 1985).

Since Savage et al.'s classic study of *American College Athletics* (1929), researchers and journalists have been studying and analyzing the structural and conflicted relationship of sports and higher education. Many of these articles, exposés and books have focused on the over commercialization and profession-alization of college sports (Chu, 1989; Thelin, 1994; Sperber, 2000; Duderstadt, 2000; Eitzen, 2000; Zimbalist, 2001; Marshall, 1994) and the lowering of aca-demic standards in undermining the educational mission of colleges and uni-versities (Bowen and Levin, 2003; Byers and Hammer, 1995; Shulman and Bowen, 2001; Simons, 1991; Simons, 2003). In *Unsportsmanlike Conduct: Exploiting College Athletes*, former Executive Director of the NCAA Walter Byers critiques college sports as a high-revenue commercial enterprise charac-terized by monetary gifts, advertising endorsements, questionable academic standards and the political manipulation of college presidents. Credited with coining the term student-athlete during the 1950s (Sperber, 1999), Byers artic-ulated an about-face, arguing that college athletes are exploited in a corrupt and commercialized system.

Several recent works by former university presidents highlight the appar-ent institutional conflict between academics and athletics. In his *Intercollegiate Athletics and the American University: A University President's Perspective*, Duderstadt (2000) argued that the commercialization of big-time college sports is at odds with the values and purpose of the university. He cited the role of the media, celebrity coaches and NCAA and conference tournaments as con-tributing factors in jeopardizing the educational mission of institutions of high-er learning. Bowen and Levin (2003) provided historical analyses of admissions data from thirty institutions to demonstrate a growing and striking advantage for recruited athletes in selection to top colleges and universities. The authors

spoke of a so-called "academic-athletic divide," defined as "the growing disjunc-
ture between intercollegiate sports and the academic core of selective colleges
and universities (219). Factors contributing to this divide, according to the
authors, included sports specialization, professionalization and the allure of
national championships. DeMott (2005) noted that "the authors frame their
discussion of the academic-athletic divide in ways that seal it off from other divisions in society itself—not only those of race and ethnicity, class and faith, but
the subtler divisions that separate excellence in intellectual activity, and
knowledge based on experience from abstract learning" (5). And in a pointed
criticism of the academics and the educators who comprise these institutions
of higher learning, DeMott continued: "Teachers who tirelessly study the com-
plexities of race, class and gender and reject crude distinctions between gay and
straight exempt the rigid categories of jock and nonjock from examination" (9).

Attempting to predict and promote the successful bridging of the so-called
academic-athletic divide, several studies have examined the relationship
between sport participation and academic performance. While some earlier
studies reported an apparent conflict between these pursuits (Sack and Thiel,
1979; Purdy, Eitzen, and Hufnagel, 1982), others seemed to suggest that athletic involvement enhances an individual's academic achievement (Rehberg
and Schafer, 1968; Schafer and Armer, 1969; Snyder and Spreitzer, 1992;
Shapiro, 1984). The inconsistency of these findings may be due in part to vari-
ations in the indicator used to assess academic performance. Such indicators
include educational aspirations and expectations, grade point average, reten-
tion and graduation rates, and post-graduation success (Snyder, 1985). However,
even when the indicator remains constant, there appear to be similar
inconsistencies.

These functional studies assume athletic participation to be a fixed variable, and therefore negate the lived and meaningful experience of embodied
actors balancing the divided terrain of intercollegiate sport. As such, the rich-
ness and complexity of these individuals' daily lives have been lost in such literature. There have been a few works, however, which have attempted to
foreground the student athletes themselves. Adler and Adler's (1987) article
and book (1991) are good examples. In their ethnographic study of a NCAA
Division I basketball team, Adler and Adler (1987, 1991) described the marked
conflict between the academic and athletic roles of the student athlete.
Through their discussion of a process they termed role domination or engulfment and the concomitant occurrence of role abandonment, these authors
found that many student athletes immersed themselves almost entirely in their
athletic role and simultaneously detached themselves from their academic

commitments. Using semi-structured interviews to examine the attitudes of female collegiate athletes, Meyer (1990) found that "the athletic subculture operated differently for the men and women" and that "the recognition males received for athletic accomplishments may have encouraged them to see themselves as athletes only." (56) Conversely, the women in Meyer's study were far more successful in balancing their athletic and academic roles.

For young men, sports may well represent what Messner (1987, 1992) described as a primary masculinity-validating experience. Messner (1987) drew from thirty interviews of former athletes to discover these men's constructions of masculinity in their interactions with sport. Within the African American community, this validation of masculinity through sport may be heightened. Edwards (1985) noted that the gendered experience of sports within the African American adolescent culture exists primarily because "the black male in American society has been systematically cut off from mainstream routes of masculine expression such as economic success, authority positions, etc." (374). The corresponding over-representation of black athletes in certain (i.e., dominant) sports has led to the celebration of black athleticism as a natural phenomenon (Entine, 2000). Debunking theories of racial athletic aptitude, Hoberman (1997) argued that this African American sports fixation has had major social implications in the United States. Of particular note is the perpetuation of the mind-body divide and the educational implications for black youth. Hoberman claimed that a fixation on sports was destructively fostering anti-intellectual attitudes among African American youth while feeding white stereotypes about inverse relationships between brains and brawn. But, according to Majors (1990), black males actually resisted institutional racism by adopting a kind of body aesthetic, characterized by "expressive and conspicuous styles of demeanor, speech, gesture, clothing, hairstyle, walk, stance, and handshake." (111) This aesthetic, or what Major refers to as "cool pose," is often most pronounced in the realm of sports.

In $40 Million Dollar Slaves, New York Times columnist William Rhoden (2006) argued that despite the fame, fortune and tremendous achievements of black athletes in the United States today, these men and women have little to no power in the multi-billion dollar sports industry. Rhoden compared today's African American athletes to indentured slaves of the past, arguing that the primary difference is that today's black athletes bear responsibility for their own enslavement. Whether the black community or black athletes themselves bear some of the responsibility for an overemphasis on athletic performance, the argument itself is part of a larger social discourse of division, the division of mind and body, of black and white, of male and female, and of sport and school.

Out of Bounds adds new insights to this discourse. It does so from the vantage points of the lived experiences of six people who have been outstanding yet thoughtful practitioners as both athletes and academics. One of the strengths of this work is that its description and analyses are across time, race, class, and gender as well as across different levels of sport and school practices. It reveals how important aspects of these arenas are really not (and should not be) fixed and rigid, but rather can be fluid and permeable as demonstrated through the stories of Erin, Anne, Malo, Ernest, Derek and Tony.

· 2 ·

VERSE IN ADVERSE CONDITIONS

On Wednesday May 20, 2009, the three finalists for the next Superintendent of the Oakland Unified School District appeared at an open forum in Oakland Technical High School's auditorium. The three candidates were vying to become Oakland's first permanent, locally-appointed Superintendent since the State took control of the District in 2003. One of the finalists was Anthony (Tony) Smith, Ph.D., Deputy Superintendent of Instruction, Innovation and Social Justice in San Francisco. Before this position in San Francisco, Tony had been the Superintendent of the Emeryville Unified School District on the other side of the Bay.

In preparing for the public forum, Tony called a few old friends to check in and ground himself before the evening's event. Tony called Natu Tuatagaloa, long-time friend, college roommate and former teammate on the U.C. Berkeley football team. Tony had played offensive line for Cal and captained the team in 1989, his senior year. Natu had played defensive line. Both were four-year Lettermen. The Cal football media guide listed Tony Smith as 6'3", 285 pounds, Natu as 6'4", 265 pounds. The media guide did not note that Tony Smith was an English major; in fact, neither majors nor any other academic particulars were mentioned in the 1989 California Football Roster.[1]

Tony also called Derek Van Rheenen, another former Berkeley student athlete and recent inductee into the Cal Athletic Hall of Fame for soccer. Tony

and Derek became friends and colleagues when earning their doctorate degrees
at the University of California, Berkeley. They had arrived as first-year graduate students, both having completed their respective professional athletic
careers, seeking to become something else. What else they might become
would hinge heavily on their past, but graduate school offered an opportunity
to realize and expand their identities as potential scholars and educators. Tony
reached out to the two men as brothers, seeking confirmation and coherence
of a life identity. Poised to possibly become the chief educational officer of one
of the poorest-performing, racially-divided school districts in the state, if not
country, Tony recognized the challenge ahead. He sought the words of two old
friends who knew him best. Many friends and colleagues had discouraged Tony
from applying for this job. The political challenge and financial problems were
perhaps too great to overcome, even with great leadership. Tony had been
recruited from his former position as Superintendent of the 800-student
Emeryville School District to address San Francisco school system's racial
achievement gap. Oakland's achievement gap was even more pronounced.
According to its Annual District Scorecard for 2007–08, it serves slightly less
than 40,000 students of whom 36.4% are African American, 33.8% are
Hispanic or Latino, 15.3% are Asian, and 6.8% are white. The drop-out rate
from ninth grade on is almost 40%. Some schools do very well in the district,
while others do very poorly, reflective of the racial and class divide in this large
urban community. The disparity of educational achievement by income and
race is striking.

Tony's call to arms was also a preparation for battle, a battle not of physical force but for who might best support educational equity and opportunity in
the troubled district. It was a preparation for the evening on the basketball
courts of Oakland Tech High School, where he would articulate a vision of
social justice rather than set picks and move bodies with his size. The words
exchanged with these friends, also former athletes, offered a discourse for the
competition ahead. The discourse was a kind of game narrative with strategies
for success in achieving difficult ends. Natu and Derek were fellow warriors and
understood battle, whether symbolic or real. They knew Tony well and remind-
ed him of who he had been, who he was, and who he wanted to become.

The idea of a coherent self is a foundational element of narrative. One's
own life story is a way of organizing experience and connecting past to present,
even envisioning the future. "For in telling their stories," Rosenwald and
Ochberg (1992: 9) wrote, "individuals make claims about the coherence of their
lives. In effect the storyteller says, 'This person I am today is who I have been
years becoming.' Further, what is included and omitted from the account ren-
ders plausible the anticipated future." But the crafting of one's own story is also

a tale reflected and refracted through others' eyes. Tony's calls to Natu and Derek were an intentional effort at exposing himself as the subject of his own text and in control of his own destiny. Rosenwald and Ochberg (1992: 9) continued: "In telling our story to another we establish who that other is (the one who will understand us, forgive us, or become converted to our point of view). In turn, as the telling of the tale turns the listener into the audience required by the teller, the storyteller's identity is reaffirmed or even altered." Thus, the making of a coherent life story is a central feature of identity, or what Erikson (1968) described as the "subjective conviction of self-sameness over time."

Postmodern critiques of such coherence in self- and meta-narratives suggest that the construction of universalist stories tends to order and homogenize difference and the plurality of different stories or identities. As Lyotard (1984) argued, "metanarratives operate through inclusion and exclusion as homogenizing forces, marshalling heterogeneity into ordered realms; silencing and excluding other discourses, other voices in the name of universal principles and general goals" (Storey, 1993: 159). The recognition of multiple identities (Ferdman, 1990) or discourses (Gee, 1990; Robinson, 1999) at play within the same individual further complicates this tendency towards coherence. These identities or discourses include class, race, gender, sexual orientation, ability, disability, among others, and underlie the ways in which people engage the social world and the way the world acts on individuals (Robinson, 1997; Winslade et al., 1997; Monk et al., 1997; Drewery & Monk, 1994). As Gee (7) wrote, "The various Discourses which constitute each of us as persons are changing and often are not fully consistent with each other; there is often conflict and tension between the values, beliefs, attitudes, interactional styles, uses of language, and ways of being in the world which two or more Discourses represent. Thus, there is no real sense in which we humans are consistent or well integrated creatures" (author's capitalizations). This does not mean, however, that people do not try to create a certain coherence to their lives. Fractured, often conflicted, individuals seek to balance these disparate discourses in their daily lives. And they do so through the stories they tell themselves and others.

The following evening, Anthony Smith, Ph.D., became Superintendent of the Oakland Unified School District by unanimous vote of the seven-member school board. His life was about to take another turn, providing reflection of where he had been, where he was now and where he was heading.

A Boy in a Man's Body

Tony's own relationship to school was framed largely by his social class/family background, his size as a child and his relationship to the sport of football. None of these factors seemed to support the development of an academic identity, at least within the institutional school setting. In many ways, these interconnected sites of physical and social space reinforced a conflicted relationship with school.

Tony wrote, "my parents were very young when I was born and they didn't stay together long." He went to ten different schools before reaching high school, moving between Stockton, San Jose, and Sacramento, California. He lived alone for part of the year when he was in the fifth grade, a ten-year-old boy at that time living in the foothills of the Sierras in the northern California town of Placerville. He survived on food stamps and walked himself to school each day. Some days he just didn't go. He wrote, "Growing up, I was larger than all the kids in my age group....By the time I was in sixth grade I was six feet tall. In eighth grade I had a full beard." A boy in a man's body, Tony seemed destined to play football. Everyone told him so. He was certain that he would play in the National Football league (NFL). Those around him at the time convinced him that this was a realistic goal. Tony wrote, "Everybody would ask me where I was going to play college football. By the end of the eighth grade I decided I would get a scholarship to Notre Dame. So, whenever anybody asked what I was going to do I would tell them, 'I am going to play for Notre Dame and then the (Oakland) Raiders or the (Green Bay) Packers.'"

Still in eighth grade, the local high school football players would pick him up after school and buy alcohol for the evening. Tony Smith's introduction into the football subculture had begun in earnest. Despite "knowing" that he would attend college, supported by those around him in this small northern California town, it was his identity as a football player that would determine his choice of institution. And the colleges and universities would come to him, recruit him to play football for their team. He received his first letter of interest the summer before his sophomore year of high school. Years later, upon reflection, Tony wrote, "My participation in athletics was my way out of a small town and a small life that would have been mine had I stayed....Without the avenue of an athletic scholarship I would not have been able to get out of my town. The only other real option would have been the military."

In junior high school, Tony had already recognized the value of his physical presence and bought into his own commodification as an athlete. He wrote, "I saw athletics as the most direct shot at the top. I was going as far as my body would take me." In many ways, his high school as educational institution is at least passively, if not equally, implicated in this athletic commodification. After his first high school football game one Thursday night, Tony did not make it to school until after lunch the next day. He had to report to the Vice Principal's office. Inquiring as to why Tony was late, this freshman big man on campus told the high school administrator "we beat the shit out of our archrivals and I was too tired to make it to school this morning. And I guarantee as long as I'm here we will never lose to them!" The Vice Principal's response tells a tale of institutional ambivalence, celebrating school pride and masculinity while simultaneously allowing for lowered academic standards. He simply said, "O.K., just try to make it before lunch." Tony's ability to work the system, while swaggering through school corridors beyond institutional reproach, promoted an academic identity that mocked the institution itself. It was an identity based on the scam. As Tony reports, "I scammed every test and cut every corner. Proving I was smarter by doing it my way." But because he represented the institution as a successful athlete, winning games and bolstering school pride, this jock identity would be tolerated, celebrated even. Unlike burnouts or other students resistant to the conservative school culture, athletes who participate on institutionally-sponsored teams support the school's broader identity in the community. And because these students do the bare minimum academically, it makes sense that they feel successful, even smart, if remaining merely eligible to play their sport. While these athletes may be disengaged academically, their role in fostering school and community pride through sport secures a privileged place in the social hierarchy and geography of the high school culture. Their popularity within this culture, as evidenced by their participation in, and recognition at, other extracurricular events, such as assemblies and dances, reinforces their affiliation with the school. As Eckert (1989: 180) argued, "Extracurricular activities provide a means by which students can grasp the institutional structure of the school. These activities combine with the administrative structure of the school to provide a hierarchical organization within which individuals can identify themselves in terms of their roles and their organizational relation to other role holders."

  While many educational institutions bear witness to, and responsibility for, this school-sanctioned academic disidentification of many of its students, many teachers and administrators also seek to bridge this school/sport divide. The very prominence of this divide may, however, place greater attention on certain students over others. The desire to deconstruct the dumb jock stereotype may leave less visible those students who are physically, and therefore symbolically, less visible. While Tony won numerous athletic accolades in high school, including being voted among the top offensive linemen for the Best of the West team, he was also honored as the English Student of the Year at the senior high school assembly. The principal herself handed Tony the award. This academic honor bestowed upon perhaps the top athlete in the class was a symbolic gesture. It was likewise an indictment of the institution's own reification of the Cartesian divide, suggesting that the acts of the mind and expressions of the body may both be rewarded, even in the same person. It was a political statement made in a high school auditorium.

Awarding Tony Smith the English Student of the Year conveyed a powerful message to this conflicted student athlete: you are more than your big body, rendering punishment on the gridiron. You are thoughtful, bright, articulate. Your potential reaches beyond playing fields. It spoke to the boy trapped in a man's body, vulnerable and afraid. That Dr. Tony Smith would discuss his vision for a troubled Oakland School district in another high school auditorium over twenty years later demonstrates just how far his body and his mind had taken him. This big kid had learned to read early and he read to escape his difficult circumstances. As Tony wrote, "all I didn't have elsewhere offered itself to me on one simple condition, that I read. In *Bullfinch's Mythology* I was lost and found myself living like Icarus. On borrowed wings I soared away from a lonely prison. In fifth grade I lived alone. I started a relationship with Emily Dickinson then. I have been with her ever since. From poems of a young boy to poems of a young poet, I have written to her for years. Through grade school, high school, college (my senior thesis was on Emily), defining moments in my life have been written." Like many others before him, Tony found solace in the written word.

These words resonated with the other members of the *Out of Bounds* group. Derek described Tony as "writing verse in adverse conditions." Jabari noted "the interesting absence of the mom and presence of an imaginary woman" in Emily Dickinson. Ernest spoke poignantly about Tony's own struggles with understanding his exercise of the mind and body and of reading and writing as escape. Ernest stated, "as a student you scabbed and you cut corners, but as an athlete you were this hard worker. And part of it was because you said that you were trapped physically, and in your need to be accepted physically you were doing things that your mind was saying you're selling yourself." bell hooks (1999: 47) described her own journey as a young and emerging writer: "writing was a place where I could leave behind the ordinary mundane pain of my life. Imagination allowed me to move through and beyond this pain...I thought then that my destiny could be just like Emily Dickinson's. I could stay alone in my little house and write. Of course as a young girl believing in magic I did not think in concrete terms about how I would acquire the house, the means to survive. I thought it would happen like magic. I let no one dissuade me from my dream of becoming a writer."

But although Tony Smith shared an affinity for the written word with bell hooks, his destiny was not to be like Emily Dickinson, at least not initially. It was to be a college and professional football player. And despite the public accolades as a gifted high school English student, Tony continued to develop his academic identity based on getting by in the classroom. In his own words, he describes his college experience as "five years of lifting weights, partying, playing football and staying eligible." And yet, he declared English as his major in college and ended up writing his senior thesis on Emily Dickinson. As the intersubjective discourse around Tony past and present continued, Tony reflected on his own words and the commentary of the other members of the group. He stated during one of the *Out of Bounds* meetings in 1997, "Something that we haven't touched on, and it's crucial is that I had no other way. I had no net, no nothing....So it was like, play football and get out or go in the army and stay there and go to jail pretty much. I didn't have the, I hate to use the word, luxury, and I could say shit like that because I was good enough and I worked harder than anybody else. I reread my bio, and it's funny that I wrote—lift weights, party, play football. It was like I had this other training, and getting ready to play the game was more important to me than playing the game. We had this whole culture of showing up at 4:30, 5:00 in the morning, we'd party all night, then go in and train, and then go home and sleep until practice. So it was just this thing that we did, the training of it, and being that guy that brought everyone together, that was when I was recruited. You know those bios that they wrote about you, mine was hard worker, known for his leadership abilities and those were like the blurbs. And basically it was because I had to, because if I didn't, I didn't know where else I would go. I mean, we could talk about it all day, but without my body, I would have been nowhere and that's the way I figured it. That this mind stuff was luxury, but I had to work and that was what I had to do. And it is interesting, the notion that the harder I work the more alienated it became from me, which is exactly a Marxist interpretation. But also the fetishization of the commodity, it becomes this thing that I am trying to build, and make and sculpt and make into this really....By my senior year, I was the iron bear, the strongest guy on the team and all that stuff. And those were the pinnacles I set, these pillars for this body and to be known that I was goofy or whatever cuz I wrote poetry, you know how they always do those specials in the paper or whatever....So it was this really touchy presentation of the body and what I was thinking and doing on the side. Very separate those things, and maybe that's why my work now focuses on mind and body dualism and finding those....Cuz I experienced it so in the extreme, and only now in excavating it and hearing from you guys and the dialogues is it clear to me really how separated those experiences were."

As Tony talked through these painful memories, he embodied this very struggle between school and sport. He was playing out the process of becoming a scholar, switching code between the language of sport and the lingua franca of the academy. His connection to Marx and working through the fetishization of his own body was strangely juxtaposed with the comfort of colloquialisms of "cuz" and a pounding of the chest for emphasis. He was learning a language to describe his experiences. The idea that Tony believed that the exercise of the mind was a luxury, a privilege of "thinking and doing on the side" demonstrates a similar alienation from his identification of being a student in an educational institution which primarily saw him as a football player. Despite his major, Tony's writing of verse was separate in many ways from the institutional requirements of school, particularly for a scholarship athlete seeking to simply remain eligible to play. He did not conceive of his collegiate football experience as play. It was work in the form of manual labor. He was training his body to be used for sport. This big strong body was his ticket out of a small town, out of poverty and limited opportunities. It was clear that he separated his body from his mind, but he also separated his mind for its official and unofficial uses. He was going to do just enough in school to get by and he would make his reading and writing of verse his own; like bell hooks, it was where he could move through and beyond his pain.

While his own performance in the classroom did not meet his academic potential as defined by the university, he created an identity as a poet warrior, a sensitive soul in an armored shell, a skilled writer and football player. Although he muddled through the academic requirements for the major, he became the informal tutor to the football team. He wrote, "When a paper had to be written the night before or the day it was due, I would whip something up for the appropriate exchange. Without any money other than my scholarship, I was making it the only way I knew—using and abusing the system." He also wanted to help his team where he could; and he could write well. Just as he took part in the commodification of his body to play football, he likewise sold his skill as a writer to help his teammates navigate the academic rigors of the university. These decisions to work the system became a badge of honor rather than an indictment of a missed educational opportunity or perceived low ability, "proving I'm smarter by doing it my way." He was getting over by simply getting by. If anything, these decisions challenged the lofty ideals of the academy, reducing school to a game, no more. Further, the university was big business, filling open seats in large lecture halls. Students were pawns in this game, just as athletes were used to fill seats in the stadium on Saturdays. It wasn't that the academy was pure and athletics corrupt; the institution needed these bodies to fulfill its mission, whatever that might be. Teaching. Research. Public Service. Fielding a winning football team. Cultivating donors.

Body Discourse in Sport and School

In both the classroom and on the playing field, the body functions as a medium for discipline and dominance. That is, the body is a medium of expression, controlled and restricted by the social structure (Douglas, 1978). Educational institutions, while reifying the division of mind and body, likewise train both the physical and pedagogic body. As Watkins (2005:3–6) demonstrated in her study of the New South Wales education system in Australia, "the school's intention to 'cultivate habits of thoughts and action' could be read as a form of institutional control leading to the production of docile bodies....The pedagogic goal, therefore, was not simply for a child to acquire a body of knowledge but a knowledgeable body: that they had habituated the skills necessary for academic success." Such Foucauldian analyses of the body within education (Goodson and Dowbiggin, 1990; Jones, 2000; Kamler, Maclean, Reid and Simpson, 1993; Marshall, 1996) are certainly not limited to any one location or type of educational institution. The hidden curriculum seeks to train a docile mind and a docile body to make obedient citizens, with the stated curriculum to energize and excite a freedom of thought and avail possibilities of social mobility.

Thus, the body is understood to be both a physical "natural" entity as well as a social representation. Bourdieu (1978) acknowledges that the body structures how we act and how we perceive the world. It is through the body that the self acts on the world, or what Csordas (1989) referred to as "embodiment." This notion of the social body has led theorists to seek to transcend the distinction of self as subject and body as object, drawing attention to the role of the body in social action (Reischer and Koo, 2004; Merleau-Ponty, 1962; Haraway, 1991; Lock, 1993; Scheper-Hughes and Lock, 1987; Turner, 1994; Wacquant, 1995). Reischer and Koo (2004: 298) differentiate between the "symbolic body" and the "agentic body," where the first "focuses on the representational or symbolic nature of the body as a conduit of social meaning, whereas the second highlights the role of the body as an active participant or agent in the social world." The symbolic body comes to be seen or read as a signifier or text of the social world, reproducing and resisting dominant cultural meanings. Thus, Michael Jordan can be viewed as a seminal cultural text, availing "avenues of agency and resistance especially to black youth who make symbolic investment in Jordan's body as a means of cultural and personal possibility, creativity and desire" (Dyson, 65). But while Jordan's body projects black cultural desires to move beyond limits and attain greatness, so too does his athletic body become a "site of commodified black cultural imagination" (70). In fact, as Dyson argued, "the black male body, which has been historically viewed as threatening and inappropriate in American society (and remains so outside of sports and entertainment) is made an object of white desire to domesticate and dilute its more ominous and subversive uses" (70). Dyson acknowledges the contradictory meanings embodied in this iconic black athlete, demonstrating how individuals actively participate in the dominant culture through consumption and production. This market is unstable, though, as cultural meanings are produced, consumed and re-produced through the commodification of sports and iconic athletes such as Jordan.

Thus, Dyson wrote, "Jordan represents the contradictory impulses of the contemporary culture of consumption, where the black athletic body is deified, reified and rearticulated within the narrow meanings of capital and commodity. But there is both resistance and consent to the exploitation of black bodies in Jordan's explicit cultural symbolism, as he provides brilliant glimpses of black culture's ingenuity of improvisation as a means of cultural expression and survival" (73). While Jordan's body is "inscribed" and "read" as a cultural text, the athlete himself is seldom seen as an agent of his own making, a physical body in motion but not a conscious body in meaning. While Dyson acknowledged Jordan's involvement in his own cultural production of meaning, repudiating "the athlete as naïf who loses his money to piranha-like financial wizards, investors and hangers-on" (70), there remains a sense of academic superiority in reading the athlete as text, divorcing the individual from his own body. There is also a corresponding implication that the athlete as native does not have the requisite proficiency to read the deeper meaning of his or her own play.

Willis (1990) is particularly helpful here, as he differentiates between material consumption and the creative, symbolic work inherent in consumption. He wrote, "human consumption does not simply repeat the relations of production and whatever cynical motives lie behind them. Interpretation, symbolic action and creativity are *part* of consumption" (21). Willis referred to this creative process of consumption as grounded aesthetics, a rebuke to formal 'aesthetics,' where 'ordinary people' actively engage and create within the dominant and dominating structures of society. Like Huizinga's (1950) notion of the play spirit in society, grounded aesthetics for Willis "are the specifically creative and dynamic moments of a whole process of cultural life, of cultural birth and rebirth" (22). Thus, Willis argued that the daily consumption of popular or common culture is potentially active, agentic, productive. Willis stated, "Crucially, we need to recognize that consumption of cultural commodities involves its own process of production...in a way that is not true for other commodities. In short, a pop song is not a steel ingot." And like a pop song, sports provide a set of activities and resources in which individuals and groups consume and produce symbolic as well as physical meanings. In this regard, Willis noted, "the body is a site of somatic knowledge as well as a set of signs and symbols. It is the source of productive and communicative activity—signing, symbolizing, feeling" (11). In the cultural practices of sport, then, the body is both instrumental in expressing physical action and also symbolic in expressing social meaning. These social meanings are inscribed on the body as the athletic body acts in prescribed ways governed by physical laws/limitations and social rules/regulations. In competitive sport, the cultural body is often read and understood in terms of performance outcome rather than in ways in which individuals experience and enjoy their bodies (Coakley, 2008). In sport, John Wilson (1994) argued, "social identities are superimposed upon physical being. Sport, in giving value to certain physical attributes and accomplishments and denigrating others, affirms certain understandings of how mind and body are related, how the social and natural worlds are connected. The identity of the athlete is not, therefore, a natural outgrowth of physicality but a social construction....Sport absorbs ideas about the respective physical potential of men versus women, whites versus blacks, and middle-class versus working-class people. In doing so, sport serves to reaffirm these distinctions" (37–38). In the construction of an athletic identity, the performative body begins to take primacy. And while the athlete determines the mobility of the physical body, his or her identity is structured by the social discourse of sport.

Tony's awareness of the academy's domestication of both his mind and body was the result of a low-income student and a recruited football player. Neither his mother nor his father had attended college. He had grown up poor and was uncomfortable with the lofty ideals of an elite academic institution. Tony reflected on his discomfort even when he had returned to this same institution to pursue a doctorate degree. When asked if he considered himself a scholar as a graduate student, Tony responded, "I consider myself a developing scholar. The label 'scholar' is highly charged for me. There are issues of entitlement and privilege associated with being a scholar. Part of me is resistant to claiming the title of scholar because I am unsure that I deserve it." His resistance to fully engage the privileges associated with the academy may have reflected his background of poverty. He recognized that many are not provided the educational opportunity of attending a university and cannot afford to be a part of this elite establishment. His own class background problematizes the historical white privilege of the academy, as he saw himself as not rightfully belonging. The resistance might also reflect his history as a scholarship athlete and the institution's own ambivalence about recruiting students primarily for their athletic talents. His value to the institution as a revenue-producing football player only heightened his experience as an undergraduate student. Being recruited for football also increased his self-doubt as a potential scholar.

His physical size, a body signified with desire and disdain in a space purportedly reserved for intellectual rather than physical exercise, further emphasized his being out of place. The academy's domestication and discipline of the pedagogic body recognize the difference in body shape and size. A big body, marked as representing an anti-intellectual, or at least anti-academic, identity, receives a different kind of attention, based more on dismissal than active training. There is a fear of these students perceived as interlopers within this lofty educational enterprise. They reveal the politics of expectation and privilege inherent to the academy and impose a sort of institutional self-reflection. If the interloper embodies masculine markers of size and strength, symbolically juxtaposed with a more feminine intellectual mind, the dismissal can be intentional. It is as if one cannot see beneath the armor, where a human being resides. Derek reflected on Tony's predicament within the educational institution: "his artistic talent seems exaggerated in a boy who was always big for his age, in a man destined for greatness of a bodily kind. Others seem to fear or revere this body rather than applauding the reflective mind residing within this physical space. The irony is that his body, while certainly powerful, is not his greatest weapon. It is the steel trap of his mind, in conjunction with his heart, which threatens to pierce through politics as usual and dismantle the powers that be. The gift is not combative but gentle and honest."

It was this open heart and sharp intellect that ultimately led Tony to be named the Superintendent of the Oakland Unified School District. His record of compassion, intelligence and strong leadership combined to make him the strongest candidate. However, his past as a collegiate and professional football player received tremendous purchase in the media's description of Tony. In a *San Francisco Chronicle* article dated Sunday June 14, 2009 (B3), education reporter Jill Tucker asked the new Superintendent three questions. In addition to asking him what he brings to the table and what will be his biggest challenge, Tucker asked Tony the following question: "You were the football captain at Cal while simultaneously writing your senior thesis on Emily Dickinson. Can you explain that combination?" Tony responded, "for me it made total sense. I was writing about stuff I cared deeply about and Emily Dickinson's poetry, to me as a young person, actually gave me a way to communicate and express myself, and football was the same thing. It was a place I felt most comfortable...and learned discipline. And to be a good, thoughtful writer requires discipline and practice. For me they were very similar." From writing verse in adverse condition, to tutoring teammates in writing term papers, writing a dissertation, to writing a cover letter in an application to be the next Oakland Superintendent, Tony can now reflect on himself as an integrated, balanced man. Perhaps having been the captain of his college football team demonstrated a leadership quality befitting his new position. Perhaps his large frame, previously used to protect the quarterback and move bodies to create holes for running backs to advance down the field, likewise prepared him for the educational battles ahead, at least symbolically. His sheer size suggested that Tony could bear a heavy load and move things forward. The troubled Oakland school system seemed like a formidable challenge, but there is perhaps no one better prepared than Tony Smith to tackle the challenge. Once a boy trapped in a man's body, he has truly become the scholar and educator for which he had the greatest potential. It is a new chapter in an evolving story.

Academic All-American

In a campus-wide email to all staff and faculty on the U.C. Berkeley campus, the Vice Provost of Teaching and Learning Christina Maslach wrote the following:

> Dear Colleagues,
>
> I am very pleased to announce that Derek Van Rheenen, Director of the Athletic Study Center, has been appointed to the position of Assistant Adjunct Professor in the Graduate School of Education. Derek was instrumental in creation of the MA Program in Cultural Studies of Sport in Education in the Division of Language and Literacy, Society and Culture within the Graduate School of Education. He will oversee and coordinate this program in his new role, as well as continue on as Director of the ASC.

This campus-wide announcement punctuated a path of academic achievement and confirmed Derek's own expectations of becoming a university professor. The new title came as little surprise. He had been teaching on the Berkeley campus for over ten years as a Lecturer. He had published articles, developed curriculum and co-designed a Master's Program in the Graduate School of Education. Prior to his initial faculty appointment, Derek had earned his Ph.D. at Berkeley and been awarded the Best Dissertation of the Year in

1997. Since 2001, Derek had also served as the Director of the Athletic Study Center, an academic support unit for student athletes on campus; he is acknowledged as a national leader in understanding the intersections of academics and athletics. As one fellow faculty member noted in support of his most recent faculty appointment, "Berkeley is widely recognized for the emphasis we place on the 'student' part of the student-athlete, not just in words but also in outcomes. The Athletic Study Center is a huge part of that success, and most of that credit should be given to Dr. Van Rheenen. National newspapers have interviewed him about student-athlete culture, about the academic stresses on student-athletes, and for explanations why some campuses do so much better than others at educating student-athletes. His reputation is quite strong among his peers in the professional advising community, evidenced by him being asked to lead a nationwide web conference for more than a thousand attendees."

Derek's appointment as a professor at Berkeley was perhaps of little surprise given his background. He grew up in affluent Woodside, California. As a white, upper-middle class male from a highly educated family, he had most of the characteristics and privileges commonly associated with the American university. Both of his parents had earned advanced degrees. His father was a medical doctor and on the faculty of the Stanford Medical School. His mother was a clinical psychologist. His grandmother was a poet, his sister a writer. His aunt and uncle were both college professors. Every member of his family was college educated. There was never a question whether Derek would attend college; the question was simply where he would go. His parents were fully engaged and supportive of this important educational decision. In his own words, Derek wrote, "my father and stepmother took me to visit some of the East coast universities that I was interested in. It was fall, the leaves were changing. Old brick buildings stood proud on these college campuses. Penny-loafered lads walked past me, their book bags in hand. In the distance, a group of foreign infantrymen with lacrosse sticks over their shoulders stood guard within this privileged courtyard. What was I doing here, a long-haired free bird, a naive Californian boy who sported a black bandanna when he ran up and down the soccer field? I didn't fit in. I didn't see that my own privilege reflected badly in this place. I only thought that I was better, when in fact I was scared. But I spoke with college counselors, spoke with soccer coaches who promised a good education and a competitive program. But I was still scared, scared to fail on foreign soil, scared to leave home."

At the end of the day, Derek chose to attend the University of California, Berkeley, a forty-five minute drive from his parent's home in the San Francisco

Bay Area.

As he wrote in 1997, "I decided to attend the University of California, Berkeley. It was highly respected. It was big and it was public. People warned me that it was like dealing with the DMV. It was a far cry from The Ivy League. The place was still steeped in tradition, but the burst of tie-dyed colors, the scent of patchouli, and a cacophony of dissenting voices suggested that I might still wear my black bandanna with pride. I seemed to fit better here. The soccer program at Cal wasn't too good, but eight players from the California State Soccer Team were all going to Cal. It was a building year. The coach told me that I would have a chance to play my first year, maybe even start." It was a good decision for Derek. He did start as a freshman. The team did well; they went to the NCAA tournament three of his four years and was ranked in the top twenty nationally. Derek also received numerous personal accolades, being named to the all-conference team numerous times, being named captain and MVP of the team, as well as being named Most Valuable Player of the League his senior year.

An important decision midway through his college career stands out in demonstrating Derek's continued emphasis on academics while earning these athletic honors. Rather than playing his junior year, he opted to red-shirt and study abroad in Göttingen, Germany. The decision was based on his desire to become fluent in the language and enhance his educational experience. He had majored in Political Economy, with a minor in German. His coach was not happy about the decision, nor were many of his teammates. The team had been very successful the year before and wanted to return to the NCAA tournament the next year. Derek's absence might hurt their chances to advance. But he told them that the decision was important for his education and he went abroad. Many athletes might have worried that by leaving there was no guarantee that he would have a place with the team the next year. It was certainly possible that he would lose his starting position. Upon his return, in fact, Derek was named the team captain and earned all-conference honors.

It was also during the season following his return from Europe that his parents hosted a barbecue and swim party after the Cal soccer team played rival Stanford University. The party was hosted at their spacious home in wealthy Atherton, California, near the Stanford campus. Derek reflected, "I can remember playing a big game against Stanford in Palo Alto, California. At that time, men's soccer had something like three and a half scholarships to split between current players and incoming recruits. It was always a pressure to hold on to your scholarship because the coach made you feel like you were taking away from his recruiting potential. He held the money over our heads, giving allowances but making you pay for it too. We were of course giving plenty to the program, but given the limited resources available to men's soccer, there was a feeling of guilt involved too. I can remember during my junior year when my parents hosted a party after we played Stanford. We had a big barbecue, swam in the pool. My coach looked out at the scene, smiled, and said to me, 'I know one player that won't be getting a scholarship next year'...He meant it too. The following season, my senior year, he revoked my money. I was the captain of the team, but he took my scholarship away. His reasoning was that I wanted to play, I would play for free, and my parents could afford it. Didn't I want to build the program, spend the money on some top high school prospects? Didn't I want to make it to the next level? After boycotting practice for the first few weeks, after lots of calls from him and from teammates, I came out to play. It was a great year, but I always resented him for that power move. I deserved to be on a full ride, regardless of my parents' discretionary income. I had earned it."

In the dialogic, intersubjective discourse about Derek, the other members responded to this memory and Derek's interpretation of the events. Tony stated, "It is all nested there in privilege, a notion of entitlement, that I didn't really bring up in the piece, but that I'd like to investigate a little bit. 'I deserved to be on a full ride regardless of my parent's income. I had earned it.' There is the issue of the individual claiming their own reality, regardless of where you came from, you did the work. You earned it, beyond the income, you deserved it. This issue of privilege coming from privilege, there is always the notion of entitlement, but I don't think that you are coming from that position. You worked really hard and you earned it. To me, that fractures the white notion of you being entitled to it. That also adds to the privileges and the whiteness." In his description of his friend 15 years later than these earlier remarks, Tony said, "Derek has a degree of self-determination that is uncommon and a sense of self, that beyond privilege, is a guiding force."

During that earlier dialogic meeting of the group, Jabari added: "What Tony created is there in the piece, but there is also something that lies dormant. And that is what were your responses to the misappropriations of your own worth? For example, the taking away of your scholarship, and I don't know whether this is cause-and-effect, but that people come to your home at a social gathering and then if my reading of this is right, it's like 'this guy has too much to justify us giving him a scholarship' and so that works against the notion of earning that is going on. It is like you are being penalized for something you have no control over...You are expected to do it, so the achievement gets denigrated."

This decision of revoking an athletic scholarship perhaps made Derek's own choices about prioritizing academics over athletics less conflicted. These decisions, of prioritizing school while playing competitive sports, led Derek to be named an Academic All-American, an honor he felt best summarized his identity as a college athlete. But it also led him to feel that his athletic identity and accomplishments were more highly valued than his academic accolades. He writes, "The school didn't make a big deal about it at all, didn't in fact say a word to me. It was typical of the way in which the Athletic Department had no clue about the bridge between intercollegiate athletics and academics. They were out of touch with the academic portion of student-athletes' education at the university. Their motto at that time: Keep 'em eligible, keep 'em healthy, keep on winning. I'm sure that the athletic department is much more impressed that I went on to play professional soccer than I went on to earn a Ph.D. and become a Professor." Given this sentiment, it is noteworthy that nearly fifteen years following graduation, Derek would become the Director of the Athletic Study Center. Housed outside of athletics, the mission of the ASC is to help student-athletes realize the promise of an education. Under his leadership, the ASC hosts an annual Academic Honors Luncheon, where student-athletes, like his former self, are recognized for their academic and intellectual accomplishments rather than their athletic feats.

Given his family background, what was perhaps more surprising than becoming a university professor, was that Derek would become a professional athlete after college, a career trajectory neither he nor his family ever considered as a viable option. While Tony "knew" that he would play professional football by the time he was 13, Derek was playing for a competitive Under-14 soccer team in his local community. His biggest goal concerning soccer at that age was winning the league and perhaps playing for the state championship. This is not to say that he was not actively striving to be acknowledged as a gifted athlete. Derek tried out for and was selected for the Under-16, Under-17 and Under-18 California State soccer teams. He traveled twice to Europe with soccer teams over the course of these three years. He helped his high school team win the league championship. But he did not see sport as his ticket out of the small town of Woodside. Rather, he writes, "It was a stroke of luck that I ended up playing at the professional level. While in college, there was no pro league, and even when I was drafted to play at the age of twenty-four or five, I always thought of it as a hiatus from real life. Playing professional sports for me was a prolonging of adolescence. *When I grow up*, I want to be something deemed serious, like a college professor." He also did not see his body as the vehicle for social mobility. At 6'1", 170 pounds, he was fit but could also fit in almost anywhere, whether a classroom, a boardroom or a locker room. He was not marked by his size, nor would his size physically move mountains or people. He would have to rely on more than his physical being, despite his somatic understanding of the body as sensual, tactile and powerful. He wrote, "there is a tactile grittiness and euphoria about sport which cannot be matched in the academic arena. On the other hand, intellectual play, a dynamic discussion among friends scaffolding ideas upon one another in a near manic dance of wit is euphoric in its own design, the two are distinct emotionally. I think that this has most to do with the body and/or mind as a medium of motor and emotive expression."

Derek may have rationalized that the successful commodification of his body at the professional athletic level was base, simply a physical evaluation of himself without an appreciation of his intellectual potential. He writes, "When I was playing professional soccer, I felt that I was not stimulating my mind enough. Of course now, I worry that I am not getting enough exercise, so it is a constant battle to retain a successful balance between mind and body. When I returned to graduate school, I really began to focus on developing my intellectual spirit which I believe to be at the heart of an academic identity." But this shift to greater anonymity and exercises of the mind came at a cost. Derek was losing his status as a star, despite what he deemed superficial accolades for simply playing a game. He wrote, "I decided it was time to move on with my life and embark upon a different journey. It was a difficult decision. Few people cheer when I write an academic paper. No student of mine has asked for my autograph for any reason other than adding the class."

Sport and Class

For Tony and Derek, their respective sports and class status informed their understanding of themselves as embodied athletes. As Bourdieu (1978: 832–833) argues, a sporting career, which is practically excluded from the field of acceptable trajectories for a child of the bourgeoisie—setting aside tennis or golf—represents one of the few paths of upward social mobility open to the children of the dominated classes; the sports market is to the boys' physical capital what the system of beauty prizes and the occupations to which they lead—hostess, etc.—is to the girls' physical capital; and the working class cult of sportsmen of working class origin is doubtless explained in part by the fact that these 'success stories' symbolize the only recognized route to wealth and fame." But unlike in the rest of the world, soccer in the U.S. has developed into a middle-class sport, where success stories of wealth and fame are often reserved for working-class foreign nationals who have achieved tremendous feats in their native countries. As Martinez (2008) argued, "soccer in the USA remains both a sport of middle-aged immigrant men and of middle class boys who don't need to succeed in sports in order to survive whatever adversity life has to throw at them" (239). For the college-educated American soccer player, opting for a professional career in something other than soccer seems a rational decision. In 2008, the starting salary for a professional soccer player in Major League Soccer was $12,900, hardly a rags-to-riches story of upward social mobility.² In 2009, the minimum salary was raised to $20,100. This meager salary in the U.S. premier professional soccer league can be juxtaposed with the contracts of international players in the same league such as British midfielder David Beckham (earning $6.5 million dollars guaranteed), Mexican striker Cuauhtémoe Blanco (earning nearly $3 million dollars guaranteed) and Colombian striker Juan Pablo Ángel (earning $1.8 million dollars guaranteed).

Thus, when deciding which university to attend, Derek sought a university which best combined elite academics with competitive soccer. He would not attend a school primarily for soccer or even for the best scholarship offer. His decision to attend one university over another did not appear to be contingent on cost. The family was not looking for the best deal by choosing the school that offered the most money for Derek to play soccer. In short, his physical capital was secondary to his plans for success. In taking his scholarship away from him because of his social class, there was likewise a reinforcement of this physical activity conceived as recreation or amateur college sport. Tony, on the other hand, utilized his physical capital for as far as his body would take him in football. By junior high school, he was well aware of the value associated with his body. He could not end his football career if he wished to continue his education, nor could the educational institution for whom he played college football strip him of his athletic scholarship and expect him to play. In his own mind, Tony did not have the luxury to focus on school and the development of his mind as a result of this economic exchange.

These divergent understandings of their athletic bodies, as experienced in a particular sport at a particular moment in time, reflected their class membership and the corresponding system of tastes and preferences or what Bourdieu calls "class habitus." He wrote (835): "class habitus defines the meaning conferred on sporting activity, the profits expected from it, and not the least of these profits is the social value accruing from the pursuit of certain sports by virtue of the distinctive rarity they derive from their class distinction." The preference for one sport over another suggests a relative tendency towards professionalism or amateurism. More specifically, the amateur athlete, tied to an aristocratic philosophy of sport, sees sport as fair play, a disinterested but spirited practice with no material gain. It is the foundational philosophy of both the modern Olympics and intercollegiate athletics. These early participants could literally afford the time and opportunity costs to commit to these games. The professional athlete, on the other hand, recognizes, even requires, an exchange of their athletic production for some kind of compensation. This is particularly pronounced as sport becomes a mass commodity for the consumption of many. Within intercollegiate athletics, the distinction is made between revenue and non-revenue or Olympic sports. Of course, few sports make money at the intercollegiate level; most sports lose money. Those revenue sports that often make money at the top competitive levels known as Division IA or the Bowl Series, are football, men's basketball, and to a lesser degree women's basketball and women's volleyball. Most athletic departments run operating deficits and must be subsidized by central campus. This larger economic reality does not seem to change most revenue-sport athletes' perceptions that their bodies are mere commodities for their respective sport and that their value to the university is first and foremost as an athlete, not as a student.

While all college student-athletes must be certified as amateurs in order to be eligible to compete, the revenue sports of college football and basketball are modeled on a professional sports ethic, supported by top-level sports medicine, marketing and media relations. These sports rely on athletic bodies, instrumental and exchangeable. So too the athletic, commodified body which breaks down is not only replaceable—it must be replaced. This reality of college athletics has led to numerous critics crying foul over what appears to be athletic exploitation rather than educational opportunity for heavily recruited young men and women (Rigauer, 1981; Marshall, 1994; Byers and Hammer, 1995; Zimbalist, 2001). The fact that the revenue sports of football and basketball are over-represented by students of color, particularly African American men and women, conjures up troubling parallels between the intercollegiate field of play and the contested terrain of the American plantation (Eitzen, 2000; Hawkins, 2000; Edwards, 1973; 1985). These critics seldom, if ever, champion the cause of the exploited Olympic or non-revenue athlete, despite their physical labor at sport. The social meaning attached to this physical labor simply carries no punch. These soccer, field hockey and water polo players are seen as truly amateur, while the football and basketball student-athletes are seen as professionals disguised as amateurs.

And while the commodified bodies of these athletes, whether collegiate or professional, are often racialized and gendered, there is likewise a structural yet fluid relationship between sport, social class and the body. That is, the taste or preference for amateur or professional sport is further substantiated by the individual's understanding of his or her body in practice. As Bourdieu argues (1978: 838), "it is the relation to one's body, a fundamental aspect of the habitus, which distinguishes the working class from the privileged classes, just as, within the latter, it distinguishes fractions that are separated by the whole universe of a life-style." For sport specifically, Bourdieu associates the working class with an instrumental relation to the body, a willingness to gamble with the body. All sports that involve some kind of fighting, for example, require a use of the body as a direct instrument of the sporting practice. As Chris Dundee, famous boxing promoter said, "Any man with a good trade isn't about to get himself knocked on his butt to make a dollar." Messner (1992: 82) suggested that not too many rich kids will take up boxing to earn a living. Or, as Wacquant discovered in his ethnographic study of boxers in a working class neighborhood of Chicago, there is a clear relationship between boxing and social class. As one trainer at the gym noted, "Don't nobody be out there fightin' with an MBA" (1995a: 521; quoted in Coakley, 2004: 339–340).

While there may be potential economic reward for gambling with one's body, there is often no guarantee but the discipline of enduring physical pain. It turns out that this bodily discipline may indeed have a cultural benefit for boys and men. The social gain for participating in these more physical, and at times violent, sports is the intersubjective celebration of masculinity, socially defined. This is a masculinity defined as powerful, performative and aggressive. Participation confirms a masculine identity and quiets the insecurities associated with "manning up" as a social imperative. That it requires kicking the crap out of another male to repress such insecurities is perhaps less an indictment of sport than it is of our reigning gender order. As Messner argued (203), "in many of our most popular sports, the achievement of goals (scoring and winning) is predicated on the successful utilization of violence—that is, there are activities in which the body is routinely turned into a weapon to be used against other bodies, resulting in pain, serious injury and even death." (Underwood, 1979; Sabo, 1985) Tony understood well this notion of using his body as a weapon and an instrument of punishment on the gridiron. He particularly recognized this relationship to his body, given his position as an offensive lineman. As Messner noted (1990: 206), "with the possible exception of boxing, perhaps the position in modern sport which requires the most constant levels of physical aggressiveness is that of lineman in U.S. football. Though T.V.

cameras focus primarily on those who carry, throw, catch, and kick the ball, the majority of the players on the field are lining up a few inches apart from each other, and, on each play, snarling, grunting, cursing, and slamming their large, powerful, and heavily armored bodies into each other. Blood, bruises, broken bones, and concussions are commonplace here."

In contrast to the instrumental use of the body by the working class or practitioners of "working class" sports, Bourdieu argues that more privileged classes view the body as an end-in-itself. Activities may be purely health-oriented, deferred gratification for today's hard workout; the body as an end-in-itself may also manifest itself as personal mastery of the body, sculpting and shaping the physique for self and/or others. While the urge to seek health and mastery of the body may be structured by the social demand for the body beautiful, socially and historically constructed, the very engagement of the body in this way reflects a class habitus. Of course it should be noted that the social demand for the body beautiful is experienced differently by men and women, whether working or middle class. Just as the social space of sports has celebrated masculinity, "'beauty work' has historically been the province of women" (Reischer and Koo, 298). While we may see aerobics or pilates as examples par excellence of treating the body as an end-in-itself today in the United States, Bourdieu viewed dancing as "the most accomplished realization of the bourgeois uses of the body," an activity which most treats "the body as a sign, a sign of one's own ease, one's own mastery" (840). It would be faulty, however, to rely too heavily on stable relationships and their corresponding cultural meanings between class, gender and sporting practices. Thus, an instrumental use of the body may produce a beautiful body, deemed so by social convention. There are also many uses of a well-sculpted body, connected to different types of work, with an individual's intention beyond health and merely seeing the body as an end-in-itself.

Thus, Bourdieu's analysis breaks down if we create stable and direct homologies between class habitus, one's relation to their body and a preference for more professional or amateur sports. European soccer might be conceived as a working class sport, indicative of certain tastes and preferences, such as the instrumental use of bodies laboring to achieve fame, fortune and a professional contract. Bourdieu's notion of tennis and golf as bourgeois sports in France must include soccer in the United States. Derek's pursuit of soccer in college and even at the professional level in the United States remained framed as an amateur avocation, despite being paid to play. It is clear, then, that one's relationship to their sport and the meaning they place on participation depends on multiple factors. Social class, relative uses of the body for athletic production and the corresponding constructions of gender identities are but several of these factors. So too are the cultural meanings associated with a social practice at a particular moment in time. The social and cultural meanings attached to playing soccer in the United States, then, are distinctly different than the meanings of playing futbol (soccer) in Europe, South America or elsewhere. To be sure, these differences are connected to who plays the sport as youth, their class affiliation, sex, etc., but also the development of the sport historically as a mass commodity (or not) with particular fans (i.e., who watch the sport as spectators), their particular class affiliations, sex, etc.

Despite this criticism of universalist structural patterns and a call for a greater plurality of meanings, there is indeed something to the proposed homologies connecting class and sport and the participants' relationship to their bodies. The social meaning attached to these working class bodies combines physical development of size and strength with heightened masculinity. But so too do these connections construct a dualistic notion of the less developed mind. The contradictory and binary construction of mind and body juxtaposes displays of physicality with those of the intellect. Within our educational institutions, the successful use of the body in and through sports, particularly those sports which emphasize power and aggression, often presume an academic deficiency. The social preoccupation with sports may therefore appear as an assault on education and more formal training of the mind. Hoberman (1997) framed this in racial terms, when he argued that public celebrations of a superior black athletic body within society at large and within the African American community itself have promoted a corollary belief in an inferior black intelligence. While celebration of the black athletic body may be more pronounced in American spectator sports today, the overly simplistic division of mind and body exists as a cultural narrative regardless of racial classification. As a poor white football player from a small town, Tony embodied this divide. The reverence for the size of his body enhanced the social separation from his own intellectual growth. His experience playing sport in school further institutionalized this divide.

Ironically, it was the finality of the breakdown of Tony's body through athletic injury that coincided with the development of a more scholarly identity. Tony went as far as his body would take him, but these injuries forced him to end his football career. In his first game as a true freshman in college, he tore the ligaments in his left thumb so he was a medical redshirt with four years of athletic eligibility remaining. As a senior, preparing for the NFL, he broke his ankle and that left him a free agent. Tony recalls, "I went to [the] Green Bay [Packers] for good money and blew my shoulder in a practice game against Cleveland. A year on IR [injured reserve] and I was ready to try again. I signed with San Francisco and in the last mini-camp tore ligaments in my right little finger and broke open a knuckle capsule. I was released in Fall camp. Stunned, I wondered 'what next?'" Tony Smith was 24 years old and his short-lived professional football career was over. Tony lamented that what his body had been trained and socialized to do could no longer be done. He acknowledged that the sport of football did not allow him the space for continued participation recreationally, even if his body was able. Tony writes, "Giving up competitive sports has been a challenge. I believe this feeling of 'giving up' competition is felt most acutely by football players. When competition is over, it is simply over. Participants in other sports still have the benefit of pick-up games or individual activity."

In juxtaposition, Derek ended his professional career on top of his game, at 28. Injuries had not hampered his decision to continue playing. The U.S. professional league in which he played folded in anticipation of the 1994 World Cup, hosted in the United States, and the establishment of a new professional league, Major League Soccer (MLS). When the old league ceased operations, Derek was the captain of the reigning national championship team, the San Francisco Bay Blackhawks. He was also a first-team league all-star. He opted to end a successful professional career rather than wait for the new league to begin. Unlike the finality of Tony's dramatic turn away from American football, Derek continued to play competitive soccer well beyond his professional career. As an indication of the blurred lines between amateur and professional soccer in the United States in the late twentieth century, Derek was a member of the last amateur team to win the United States Open Cup in 1994, soccer's most elite and longstanding national competition. Since then, only teams in the professional league of Major League Soccer have won this coveted title. Derek played on three additional national championship soccer teams, two at the Over-30 division (1996, 1998) and one at the Over-40 division (2004). Like Bourdieu's analysis of golf and tennis as bourgeois sports in Europe, Derek's experience with soccer in the U.S. provided a space for a middle-class male to experience sport as a lifelong competitive amateur avocation. His continued play likewise demonstrated what Tony had lamented about the forced finality of his own athletic competition.

Turning to Reveal Oneself

Derek's turn from professional sport to the academy may have seemed like a logical move given his class background and his family's emphasis on education, but the turn was likewise choreographed to allow for his own increased mobility. If the space of sports celebrated raw masculinity and compulsory heterosexuality, the academy heralded the intellect and a freedom of expression, so often characterized as feminine. The social mobility Derek sought with this move was not one based solely on class structure and increased economic opportunity. This was also a move to more publicly align his projected new professional life with his emerging sexual identity, to reveal and become more whole. But this process was tremendously slow, fraught with risk, discomfort and pain. But in this stepping out of bounds, Derek also sensed the potential gain in becoming more than he had been.

While playing professionally, Derek hid the fact that he lived with a man—not as a roommate or a teammate—but as his lover. As the captain of the team, he was all business on and off the field, because that's what being a leader called for, but it was also because he kept his private life separate. Like so many athletes before him, it was safer to remain closeted, a part of, while apart from the team. In varying degrees, sport allowed the space for intersecting identities. At times, these intersecting identities become integrated. But even when the male locker room is not overtly homophobic, there often remains the expectation of desire, a physical, sexualized attraction to the opposite sex. This compulsory heterosexuality limits the freedom of genuine expression for gay male athletes in these sporting contexts as they either play along and pass (for straight) or confront this culture of expectation. Because the male jock identity so effectively supports the larger social construction of masculinity, openly gay male athletes weaken the structural stability of the reigning gender order, especially if they embody the characteristics constructed around hegemonic masculinity. As Messner notes, (1990: 205), "hegemonic masculinity—that form of masculinity which is ascendant—is defined in relation to the subordination of women and in relation to other (subordinated, marginalized) masculinities."

Derek reflected on a time in college when he told a male friend that he thought that he might be gay: "my friend would not hear of it. He just couldn't fathom that this big man on campus, the captain of a Varsity team, could possibly be queer. He just shook his head and said 'no.'" But, as it turned out, Derek was gay; his return to the academy to become a scholar was also about becoming more comfortable with his sexual identity. The intersection of these emerging identities in fact helped steer the course of his scholarship. He came to understand that there are many masculinities and that the notion of gender and sexuality are far more open and porous social categories than rigid understandings of being male or female, being gay or straight.

Derek's research would combine his emergence as a scholar and as a gay man. His identity of becoming something else other than merely the jock was also about coming out, a narrative turn of lasting consequence. In one of his publications, "Boys Who Play Hopscotch: The Historical Divide of a Gendered Space" (2000), Derek demonstrated how the simple lines of a children's game have served to separate boys from girls, institutionalizing the binary construction of gender and sexuality in the twentieth century. He wrote, "once a game played predominantly by boys, hopscotch has undergone a historical transformation in both the gender of play participants, as well as the cultural meanings attached to its gendered involvement. Thus, within the 20th century, the socially constructed space of the hopscotch diagram has come to be marked as feminine, a cultural text inhabited primarily by preadolescent girls. Boys who play hopscotch today run the risk of being deemed effeminate, a stigmatized marking in a patriarchal society" (112).

This notion of patriarchy, however, should be understood as more than simply male power and privilege at the expense and exclusion of women (Connell, 1987; Carrigan et al., 1987). As Messner argued (1990: 205), "not only does the concept of patriarchy tend to view 'men' as an undifferentiated category, it tends to downplay the fluidity and contradictions that exist within and between gender categories." Derek had begun to explore this fluidity in his research and writing, coming to terms with the apparent contradiction of being a gay male athlete.

Like his friend Tony on a similar but different journey of self, like Emily Dickinson and bell hooks before them, Derek had found solace in reading and writing. He spoke out to announce his coming, wrote to articulate where he was going. His narrative turn looked at history, sought perhaps where he and other like boys had been. As Tony had written of his own boyhood, "on borrowed wings I soared away from a lonely prison." The quote spoke to the experiences of all of the informants in the *Out of Bounds* group. In some ways it revealed the space of sports and school and how these institutional spaces became bound, limiting, alienating. But the very structure and geography of these spaces likewise provided a clarity of rules and norms and the subsequent risks and rewards associated with stepping outside of these boundaries. The way in which these men and women crossed lines of demarcation was not unlike children in a hopscotch diagram. Their agility to navigate spaces at once confining likewise promised a playfulness of movement. While certain spaces limit mobility, others provide safety to soar. Individuals move in prescribed ways but turn intentionally to announce their individuality. The lived stories of Tony and

Derek as athletes becoming scholars and educators illustrate that seemingly static social categories of race, class, gender and sexuality are in fact fluid. We are limited by the structure and rules of the game but we may play freely nonetheless.

Notes

1. Twenty years later, little has changed. In the 2009 Cal football media guide, there is at least mention of each student-athlete's major or projected major. It is the last sentence under a heading entitled Personal, which follows the player's picture, football position, physical statistics (height and weight) and hometown. The bulk of the bio focuses on the student-athlete's football accomplishments to date. It is a football media guide, after all, but the student accomplishments are glaringly absent.

2. Rags-to-riches stories through sport are rare in major spectator sports, but achieving the American Dream through professional soccer is nearly impossible in the United States. Of the 359 players listed by the MLS Player's Union in 2008, 55 earned $12,900 and an additional 35 earn $17,700. Nearly all who earn these paltry salaries are journeymen or developmental American players. For more on the development of soccer in the United States, see Van Rheenen's "The Promise of Soccer in America: The Marking and Open Play of Ethnicity in the San Francisco Soccer Football League (SFSFL)," *Soccer & Society,* 2009. This article juxtaposes the perceived lack of success of professional soccer in the United States with the nation's rich history of ethnic and amateur soccer. The author argues how soccer as ethnic subculture has provided a means for ethnic communities to both construct a unique cultural identity while becoming a part of an emerging multicultural nation.

· 3 ·

SLAVES OF SPORT

Ernest made a statement about sport in one of his written reflections in 1997 that resonated with all of the participants in the *Out of Bounds* group. He wrote, "I know that I was used by the university and the athletic department not only as an athlete, but as a poster boy....My mother once came to a track meet, and seeing that I was the only one participating in so many events, asked the coach if he knew that slave labor was over." The cultural and political space between being used as a poster boy for the university and being used as a "slave" of sport by the athletic department marks the field of play and goals of this chapter.

Rhoden, the *New York Times* columnist, claimed in *$40 Million Dollar Slaves* (2006) that in terms of real power, black athletes were comparable to slaves in America's past, except that contemporary athletes bore responsibility for being in this position. These images and claims are provocative, yet they continue dichotomous portrayals of black bodies and sharp minds. This chapter uniquely explores how and why the games of sport and school were able to enact the poster boy and the slave, and how our collaborators/informants were submitted to and resistant to both in ways that forged the construction of identity and masculinity. It illuminates the roles and influences of significant people in our participants' lives like their coaches, team members, teachers, professors, parents, peers, and friends. It also explores critical moments when a decisive turn was made from the play of sport to other life and career choices. We do this through insights from extended dialogues that centered on the stories and personal reflections of Ernest Morrell and Malo Hutson, African American men who were outstanding athletes and also became distinctive stars in academic fields.

We note the significance of the work of Kenneth Stampp, the influential 19th century historian and Berkeley professor emeritus who died on July 10, 2009 at 96. His important counter assessments of the motives and meanings of U.S. slavery, the Civil War, and Reconstruction debunked the propagated characterization of slavery as a necessary institution by documenting the voices and actions of enslaved Africans rather than depending only on the views of their enslavers. Importantly, he described many ways that blacks resisted slavery from work slow-downs and property destruction to armed uprisings. We have also raised the voices of our collaborators/informants on their experiences as "slaves" of sport and students in school—voices that sound notes of both harmony and discord.

Reflections

Like Ernest, Malo wrote in one of his personal reflections of feeling like he was treated like a slave in his sport of baseball. Ernest indicated how his mother had challenged his coach on how many events he was asked to run, and Malo's mother was similarly attentive to ways that sport might exploit her son. In fact, Malo wrote, "The main influence in my life has been my mother. My parents divorced when I was almost four years old, so I have only had contact with my mother and not at all with my father." While growing up his mother encouraged him to play sports, but also to always get good grades in school. Doing both was never a conflict for him until he started high school.

Malo recounted how on the first day of high school registration, he and his mother were "tracked down" by the school's football coach. The coach caught up with them as they were heading to the parking lot after registering and asked Malo if he wanted to play football for him. He told Malo and his mom that he could definitely get him into college on a football scholarship, and that he should not "put all [his] eggs in one basket," implying that he should not depend solely on academics to get into college. Malo noted, "My mother and I were furious at the coach's approach." He later found out that this coach had tried to get every African American male at the high school to play football, and he persisted in trying to recruit Malo every year.

Malo never did play football, but he did play baseball throughout high school. Yet, he found his baseball coach to be just as bad as the football coach when it came to promoting sports over academics. For example, when Malo was a junior and it was time to start inviting college coaches and scouts to come and watch him play, his high school coach told him to make a list of all the colleges he was interested in attending. When Malo gave him the list with universities like Princeton and Berkeley on it, the coach said that these were really good schools and then put the list away. "Despite taking all honors and advanced placement courses throughout high school," Malo wrote, and being "president of my high school's National Honor Society, and captain of the baseball team, my coach doubted my academic potential. My senior year of high school, he kept giving me college brochures of local colleges and never contacted any of the schools I had listed the previous year."

Although Malo went on to play baseball for three years at Berkeley, he was not recruited out of high school to play there because his coach never made any of the calls or connections to get him seen by the university. Instead, he was accepted to Berkeley on an academic scholarship and later wrote to the school's baseball coach and tried out and made the team as a walk-on. "To make things worse," Malo recalled, "Once I got accepted to Berkeley, my high school coach told people he had something to do with it and if people played baseball for him, he could get them into a Pac 10 (Pacific Conference) school." Unfortunately, college baseball brought its own problems for Malo. In reflection he wrote, "We were told when to be at practice, what times our classes had to be taken, and in some cases which classes were easier to get an 'A' in, or which classes they knew the instructor. I felt like the coaches were only concerned about themselves and little about the well being of students. No matter how hard I tried to be a student-athlete, I was always viewed as an athlete only….I mainly quit because I felt like a slave."

Like Gilroy's (1993) chronotopic ship, for Malo sport had acted as a bounded space that moved inside and between society's institutionalized cultures while at the same time having a complex culture of its own. The space of sport in which he found himself was propelled by the laboring bodies of prime athletes while the hierarchical structures of power and privilege immensely benefited from their production and from the reproduction of their conditions. Through his experiences in sport, something of an x-ray of the nature and motives of forces at work within institutional cultures was revealed. The motives for what school and society wanted to produce from sporting practices did not accommodate athletes who not only worked their bodies, but also exercised their minds. The nature of these forces depended on an absence of critique and the presence of discipline—a disciplined body that accepted and celebrated the pain of labor, a disciplined mind that honored and supplicated to the hierarchy that created and enforced the rules of the game. Coaches were captains, but like the ship captains in the black Atlantic triangle, they were not the real beneficiaries of this corporeal trade. The real beneficiaries were capitalists who structured sophisticated, specular systems for exploiting the work of exceptional bodies. When Malo decided to leave this space of sport, most of those around him felt like he was blindly walking the plank on his career possibilities. Instead they would later realize, he had found a more viable vehicle for realizing his goals.

Ernest's academic achievements like Malo's were exemplary, but unlike Malo he felt his "entire image was centered on athletic accomplishments." This made him wonder later in life after he had left track competition for good, why he had never previously thought of himself as a scholar. He was valedictorian in junior high, graduated high school summa cum laude, and finished his undergraduate education with a degree in English at UC Santa Barbara with a 3.5 GPA. He surmised, "I believe it was because I have been viewed by my teachers, peers, coaches, and the community at large as an athlete first and foremost…I just considered myself to be a smart athlete." It was not until Ernest applied to graduate school that he reconceived a self-image that did not revolve around athletics. "I could truly, for once, be a scholar," he wrote and perceptively described how that identity had been negated in his earlier experiences. "There were no big crowds to cheer me on in trigonometry class, and the results on a history midterm would never make the papers," he reflected. "Besides, I was fairly large for my age (6'2" and 180 lbs.), had an athletic build, and was frequently the only black male athlete in my classes. I actually did not feel safe in any other persona than a hard-core athlete, even when in an academic class."

Ernest spoke more appreciatively than Malo of his experiences in sport and of his coaches who he said constantly drew parallels between sport and academics and sport and life. He understood what they were trying to teach—"that lessons on the field are universal and that our ultimate goal is to become All-American citizens, not athletes." But, as a youth, he viewed sports as an end and not as a means. His room was covered with sport memorabilia. "There were no pictures of Martin Luther King on the wall in my room. All my heroes were black male athletes, and all I dreamed of was sports." He didn't seriously contemplate a professional career in sport as an adolescent, but he noted that he did not develop an alternative either. He traced his ambivalence about sport and academics to situations early in his life where though he excelled in both, he noted, "But I never really felt safe in class." He explained this in the following way. "I felt like an odd ball for being smart or being advanced because that also meant to be with the white kids. With them I felt there was always something to prove, and simultaneously, I felt like I was turning my back on or losing my connections with my black heritage and my family. All the black kids who played on my sports teams seemed to disappear when the bell rang. My family began to accuse me of talking differently and some made fun of my academic success. Athletics, however, was a different matter. With one exception, all of my coaches up to high school were people of color, and my sports teams were dominated by non-white players. These were the guys I hung around with during and after school. The ones who looked like me, listened to the same music, dressed the same. And the way I earned their respect was by dunking a basketball, not by getting a 4.0 GPA."

Sadly, in addition to the denigration of academic accomplishments Ernest received from some family members and friends, his teachers also responded more to his physical presence than to his intellect. His school experience in eighth grade was a case in point. He had the best academic record in a class of nearly 400 students and was also All District in basketball and track. Yet, his teachers labeled him as having an attitude problem. He noted that he was frequently kicked out of class, and that he was generally viewed with contempt by the faculty and administration. "In class, I was alone and isolated from my peers," he wrote. "In athletics, however, I was hailed as a superstar with the opportunity to be a scholarship athlete in two sports."

Ernest reflected on how high school coaches would come to watch his games and how private schools that were athletic powerhouses called his parents and offered him scholarships. High school athletes knew him by name and would invite him to play ball with them. The men's varsity basketball coach of a noted high school team invited him to play in a summer league with the team. "If you were in my position and these two mutually exclusive domains of existence were open to you, which would you have chosen," Ernest asked rhetorically? As a young athlete who "happened to be smart," his choice was easily made. "On my 8th grade graduation day, I crossed the stage, accepted my awards, and left the ceremony early to attend a high school varsity summer league game."

Dialogues

All of the participants received and wrote responses to each other's personal reflections and these (along with transcriptions of interviews and earlier meetings) were the foci for a series of group discussions. We also read several books and articles that we recommended to each other, and ideas from them worked their way into the discussions too. In addition to Ernest, Malo, Tony and Derek, Jabari Mahiri and Mojgan Jelveh participated in all of these discussions. At times in these meetings there were other participants who were prominent scholar/athletes but did not become "focal" informants for this work although their voices are occasionally in the dialogues. Derek characterized the structure of our discussions as Jabari and Mojgan acting as coach and assistant coach for bringing everyone's ideas into dialogic play. The following presentation of the participant's ideas flows across themes and meetings, rather than adhering to the exact sequence.

As we talked, we attempted to be cautious to not reinforce stereotypes and to offer checks and balances to each other's ideas. The form of our engagement emerged because the participants saw generative value in their ideas being cross-fertilized by the ideas of other participants offering new roots and shoots of rhizomatic growth and connectivity. We were actually defining the process for our discussions as we engaged in them. For example, Ernest made the following observation in one of our initial meetings. "While we are doing these readings, can we question each other? Because one area that would be interesting for me personally is the questions that would arise from reading each other's reflections, and the self-evaluations that would come about, and the learning that happens about myself and my experiences as an athlete from reading other athletes' profiles. I mean like Jabari said about reflecting on ourselves, it could be another project just about the self-discovery that comes about from this kind of dialogue."

The experiences of Ernest and Malo were paired in these discussions, and the value of having them present and participating in the emerging, composite interpretations was evident in this process of focusing and crystallizing salient features of their backgrounds from multiple angles. Among other things, we attempted to understand why terms like "slave" and "slave labor" and continual references to exploitation and the negation of their intellects came up so frequently and worked so seamlessly as signifiers for crucial aspects of their experiences. For example, in commenting on Malo's reflection of feeling "like a slave" and on the point in Ernest's reflection about "slave labor," Derek noted that poignancy of sporting practices for black athletes in particular. "The idea of the university exploiting its athletes carries far greater punch when such exploitation involves young black men. The fact that the revenue producing sports disproportionately recruit from the African American community seems to exacerbate this issue even though, structurally speaking, this econom-

ic exploitation would seem to take equal advantage of other races and ethnic-
ities involved in these sports."

Tony addressed the exploitation of black men in sport with some discomfort initially. "I was so taken by the slave comment that at first I didn't want
to write about it. I thought I should just leave that alone," he told the group.
"But then I interrogated my own reasons behind that, and thought about going
outside my own boundaries since we are talking about stepping out of bounds....
I didn't know if this would seem like taking it too far, but for me writing about
this seemed like I was doing just what we are talking about." "I felt the same
thing as Tony," Derek responded. "That definitely spoke to me, but I didn't feel
uncomfortable discussing it because it's such a powerful topic. To leave it out
would be missing the essence of their reflective pieces—the way these issues
came out in both....But what struck me also was that Tony and I saw a lot of
the same themes. Whether that is just from the perspective of being white, I
don't know. I don't think so."

No one in the group felt that Tony was taking things too far. Jabari noted
that the slave issue had come up spontaneously in both men's statements in such
a way that we couldn't just negate it or say that they were merely using strong
or colloquial language. "We need to look at the term and see why it acts as such
a ready made place holder for how these African American men have experienced sports in schools," he said. "I don't think that it just jumped out at you
two because you are white," he noted. "As a black man, it jumped out at me
too."

As Tony continued his response to Malo's reflection, he talked about the
focus, drive, and strength of character that Malo had expressed along with the
committed support of his mother as clear reasons for why he was eventually successful beyond his sport. He also attributed Malo's quitting baseball as a result
of feeling like a slave to his strength of character. He noted, "These are powerful words for anyone, and doubly so for a young African American male.
However, what strikes me more…is the context where he felt enslaved—sport
that is offered up as the pinnacle of freedom and success." Tony concluded,
"Ironically, it was the freedom to pursue his dreams that Malo felt was being
taken away. It is a testimony to his strength of character that he never doubted his potential and that he did not allow anyone to deny him access to his
dreams. Intellectual dreams of young African American males are not nurtured
in the United States." "That's right on the money," Malo responded. "About
my mother and the idea of the slave, that is right on the money. You really
described how I felt, and my whole decision process." He talked about how
weird it felt using the word "slave." "When I was writing it, that was the only

word that described how I felt. When you use this term, it really stands out, but there was no other way to put it." He acknowledged that a lot of white athletes and athletes of other races were exploited as well, but in the U.S. this kind of exploitation could cut deeply and differently for blacks. He recalled how he and his teammates would sometimes joke about the term—"dang coach, you treating us like slaves"—but they didn't dare address the actual parallels seriously. That's why he said he was somewhat surprised when he found that Ernest had used the same term to characterize aspects of his experiences in sport.

In continuing the discussion of the slave metaphor, Ernest also sought to understand the bitterness he felt about the exploitive nature of his sport experiences. He linked his bitterness to how he saw sporting practices taking advantage of the naiveté, insecurities, and weaknesses of athletes, often starting when they were very young as in his case. "When I go back in my mind to athletics," he noted, "it isn't so much the moments in the game that I think, could I have changed something. Instead, I think about why I didn't respond differently to those things." These things had to do with ways he felt his manhood was constantly being challenged by his coaches and peers, despite the fact that he was really just a kid at the time.

As a man he still had bitter memories of his youthful insecurities and weaknesses being exploited by his coaches. When he was younger, he wasn't confident in himself, but later he also realized that confidence wasn't seen as a positive thing in an athlete. He told the group, "The coach would essentially say, 'Is he a good boy? Does he do his chores? Does he say "yes, sir" loud enough'? If you have too much confidence, then you're seen as uncoachable. So, I had my confidence coached out of me. The better I got, the more insecure I was. The more insecure I was, the weaker I got. The weaker I got, the more I was able to be exploited." It took until college for Ernest to finally be able to make this kind of critique. Coming to this understanding made it difficult for him to continue participating in sports, even recreationally. "The first time I did anything as far as sports was last year, and that was three years after I finished running track and being in the league," he noted. "Even that was weird because the bitterness around how I was commodified in sports and trying to formulate that identity. I was an athlete those first 22 years and now even after three years of being a non-athlete academics is still new." He admitted that these reactions of not participating in sports were probably overcompensating for his inability to react in the past when he didn't have an understanding of how he was being manipulated.

"These discussions make me feel less alienated that I wasn't the only one this happened to," one participant told the group. "It gives me a microphone to voice things that for a long time bothered me. It's inspiring that other people overcame the opinions of the coaches and other players that mattered so much to them." He talked about how his coach had no expectation that he could be an excellent student, how he had wanted to take a challenging class, but the coach had said no. Yet, he had cooperated with the coach's agenda and kept playing because he couldn't break out of the mindset of being an athlete first and foremost. He knew other athletes who had genuine intellectual interests but no encouragement from either coaches or teachers to pursue them. In the end, like Ernest, he became highly conflicted about his sport of soccer after he finally left it due to injury. Though he would often get invitations to play with clubs in Marin and San Francisco, he always turned them down. "I can't put on the cleats anymore," he would tell them. "It's like I can't even lace them up....I found a box with my old soccer stuff from Cal, and I just put it in the dumpster. It was like, it's over. I will never play this game again."

Mojgan pointed out that our discussions were taking a different turn in that Derek and Tony had focused on making further elaborations on Malo and Ernest based on what they had read, while the other men had used the reflections of Malo and Ernest to go into discussions about themselves. The irony of the white men staying on point, and coming to the meeting with written responses while the others were responding more in the moment was not lost. We confirmed, however, that we all were comfortable with the discussions continuing to evolve spontaneously rather than following a preconceived structure. We liked the intensity of insights that were emerging.

Malo went on to talk about how he felt free after deciding to leave baseball, but he also admitted having conflicted emotions about leaving the game that were still unresolved. "People thought it was BS, like how could you stop something that meant so much, cold turkey." He said that it wasn't until the *Out of Bounds* project started that he could really think about it. "There was too much pain and anger and frustration." The project forced him to finally sit down and reflect. He started having dreams about baseball experiences during the time of our discussions. "They always end with my coach doubting me, and they bring back the anger." As time passed he was hopeful that he could also see things from his coach's perspective. But ultimately, he didn't think he could reflect and be fair—that he might be biased forever. He admitted that more recently he had started to miss baseball. "Even then, it was from a distance," he said. "It was just like fantasizing about going up to bat one more time." He talked about going to the university's recreation center for the first time in about two years. "I can finally do it....Part of it, I think, is being in grad school now. It was like so many people doubted and wrote me off, that it is almost like vindication now. I proved them wrong, so now I don't mind going around and showing my face at the park."

Derek commented on the pain that Malo and Ernest had carried into adulthood as a result of their experiences in sport. "It could be the physical pain of blowing out an ankle, but it's really broader than that. Like it's mental and emotional pain as well, and it goes deeper. It's almost spiritual." These painful memories were most often connected to similar ways these men had been treated by their coaches. It was double jeopardy for one of our participants because his high school coach was also his teacher. "I can see now how much my coach's perceptions of my athletic and my academic abilities affected me," he said. He had asked his coach to put a videotape together to send out to recruiters, and the coach not only told him no but also snickered and told him that he was not college material. "His assessment of my playing and also of my academic ability stung me twice," he noted. The coach was seen as a professional in sport as well as a professional teacher whose opinions he valued. So, hearing the coach denigrate a player's physical and mental abilities was devastating. "There is a huge power given to coaches to make these assessments of young men, that has a large influence on how you approach school as an athlete or a scholar-athlete," he told the group.

Ernest pinpointed some of the causes of the ambivalence that he and the other men of color expressed regarding trying to play at a higher level and also be a student at a higher level. He felt it was influenced, in part, by the fact that many black players accepted being defined as athletes only by their coaches and teachers. "I had a lot of friends who were African American athletes that had no intention of becoming good students. I was the only one as far as I could tell that was trying to straddle the fence." He felt the ambivalence was there because his athletic success actually worked to preclude being seen as anything but an athlete, even in class. "I could have gotten an 'A' on a paper, but even if I scored only ten points in a game everyone would still comment about what a great game I played. When this is constantly reinforced, you never want to jump into the role of a student because it doesn't compare with the rewards of being an athlete." With so much of his identity having been invested in and rewarded by being an athlete, it was intimidating for him to walk away from all that to be just a student. "Even with all the years of academic success, not having sports there was really scary because I was doing that since I was 6 years old. And I was 22, and it was the first time that I hadn't done it. And I wasn't prepared for the insecurity I felt in stepping outside of that role to only be a student."

"Absolutely," Malo said in response to Ernest. "I had the fear of just being a nobody. With sports, no matter where you go, someone knows you....With academics, no one knows you, knows what major you're in. That was a scary thing. Without athletics, I was just exposed. What was I *really* about"? We talked more about things that factored into the ambivalence, insecurity, and fear these men experienced in turning away from being athletes toward becoming scholars. We considered whether there was a difference between seeing one-self as a "scholar athlete" versus an "athlete scholar" in terms of the significance of which word was the adjective and which was the noun. Jabari noted, "Athletes don't usually get to decide which word is the adjective or the noun. You might have a sense of which one you would prefer, but the sport and school contexts you described can make the word "scholar" not even a modi-fier or not even in the same sentence with the word "athlete."

The negation of the intellectual side and the consistency of that negation in the personal statements and reflections of both Ernest and Malo contributed to the construction of the idea of being slaves of sport. Jabari commented, "This gets us into the body. Coaches don't deal with the intellect; their objective is to exploit the capabilities of the body. Therefore, it is the thinking person that begins to say 'wait a minute.' If this question isn't raised by the African American athlete, then he is only an athlete. It is only when the intellect is exercised also that there is a possibility of the slave question coming up." Derek added to this point by saying, "It's powerful to understand that if coach-es only have the body to exploit, then highlighting the physicality of the indi-vidual for black athletes gets played up doubly in light of race."

"Additionally," Jabari noted, "inside each sport, they also make racial dis-tinctions about intellect—the smart quarterback, the white mentality versus the black physicality, making racial distinctions in the way the game is approached intellectually." Acknowledging this sociological process that is called "stack-ing," another participant continued the consideration of how these perspectives were linked to styles of play. He talked about his experiences playing on a sum-mer basketball team composed of the best players in the state at his age level. Most of these youth played what was seen as an urban style of basketball, but the coach at his school did not like that kind of game. When he played that way at his school, his coach would say that he was a reckless player who did-n't analyze the game the way point guards did who did not play an urban style. He had similar experiences in soccer in terms of his coach's preconceived notions of styles of play and preferences for what was considered to be more mental approaches to the games.

The stories of these men coalesced around obstacles and difficulties of bridging the gulf between two consuming identities. One construction of their identities worked to physicalize and racialize them in the practices of sport and school in part by challenging and channeling their emerging conceptions of masculinity through a cultural logic of dichotomies. Within this cultural logic, Tony noted, "The African American body is the repository of physicality and sexuality, not the embodiment of intelligence and reason. For one black individual to move easily in both the athletic and academic arenas created an uncomfortable friction between cultural conceptions and reality." It's clear from these men's stories that these cultural conceptions were not only held by coaches but also by many of their teachers. Ernest, for example, talked about some of his teachers in middle school and high school who questioned his being placed in their honors classes as the only black kid and an athlete on top of that. He noted that their questioning of his intellect ended up motivating him even more to get As.

Ernest's high profile status in sport and his place in a sea of white faces in the classroom gave him hyper-visibility in both arenas but with different results. It was a visibility that was accepted and promoted in one domain but resisted and questioned in the other. So when he matriculated at the university, the perception of his presence on the college campus—one of the few "brown faces"—was that he must surely be an athlete. When he was approached (as he often was) and asked which sport he played, people could not see how humiliated he felt. He could tell that the role of athlete was nearly always the only one imagined for him. "I felt like I was reinforcing stereotypes even though I knew I had as impeccable a set of educational credentials as any of my fellow students," he noted. In so many ways, the mind/body dichotomy also contributed to racial divides.

When another role was admitted for Ernest, it was that of a poster boy for the university. African American students were less than three percent of the student population at UC Santa Barbara. "That was bad enough by itself, but it's even worse when you're an athlete," he told the group. "I was used as poster boy for the cause of civil rights and equality." He described how on the track he was called upon, as a freshman, to do five events "because sprinters and jumpers are so difficult to recruit and keep eligible." Off the track, he was often called upon to make presentations and speak to incoming African American student recruits. Even the women's volleyball coach would ask him to talk to her black recruits who, according to Ernest, "often looked mortified at the scarcity of brown faces on campus." The coaches wanted him to convince them of the many opportunities the school held for athletes and other students of color. What Ernest wanted was to be recognized for more than his physical presence. He noted, "All I needed was inspiration, purpose, and support to form a nonathletic identity." But, these needs were almost never met by either his coaches or teachers.

The participants had read a number of articles and books on these issues, and ideas from these sources were brought into the discussions. We noted how the experiences of our informants corresponded to the findings of a number of scholars who analyzed how sporting practices were primary masculinity-validating experiences (Messner, 1987) that took on added dimensions for black athletes who often experienced being cut off from other avenues of masculine expression in American society (Edwards, 1985), leading to a celebration of black athleticism and the black body, on the one hand (Majors, 1990), and as Hoberman (1997) claimed an unhealthy fixation on sport by black males on the other. What our informants' stories revealed were definitive ways that specific actors and activities in sport, school, and society worked to establish and reinforce these physicalized and racialized categories and perspectives for black athletes, even when there were overwhelming indications that these men had abilities for achieving at the highest levels in professions and in society beyond the realms of sport.

We discussed particular events in society and in the lives of these men that were illustrative of a cultural logic with roots in and before American slavery that worked to reinforce and heighten the stereotypes of physicalization and even criminalization of blacks and other men of color. We saw the media particularly supporting and reinforcing these kinds of racialized perceptions and images in the American psyche. For example, we talked about the implications of an article in the *San Francisco Chronicle* (1997) that reported that "the psychological adviser...of the Phoenix Suns has determined that Atlanta's Dikembe Mutombo is the only player in the NBA to have a brain type labeled 'INTP.'" The article further stated that this is the most intellectual brain type, the kind possessed by Albert Einstein (Fitzgerald, p. C8).

We were aware of many articles like these that blatantly provided biological explanations for the over-representation of blacks in certain sports. But we also talked about how this was done in more subtle ways in newspaper and magazine articles that emphasized physical characteristics of blacks when that emphasis had nothing to do with what the article was about. We looked at the example of another *San Francisco Chronicle* article in a weekly series entitled "Classroom Chronicles" that explored education issues. Though the article was about the issue of how Bates College dealt with getting diverse, quality students without the SAT being required, we thought it was interesting how the writer characterized the four focal students that were discussed. Two were women, one Latina and the other Vietnamese, and two were African American males. In the case of the description of both of the women, the article never provided any physical descriptions. Instead, it noted what they were majoring in at college along with other academic achievements like excellent class rankings from high school. In the case of both males, however, it went into detail discussing how they looked. Mark Meados was described as "an African American with closely shaved hair and a small gold earring in each ear." It was noted that he had never graduated from high school but earned a General Equivalency Diploma. Ethan Gums, "his hair plaited into braids below his shoulders," was also described as living in East Oakland and having plans to apply to four University of California campuses in addition to Bates (Freeberg, 1993: A1).

The physical attributes that were described for Meados and Gums may be accurate even if they might also connect to images often associated with black athletes, but the question is why are these images brought into focus when they are not related to the immediate context, and when the same focus on the physical is not made for the other students who were featured? Contrast this to another article that appeared in the *San Francisco Chronicle* about two teenaged white males who were suspected of murdering two Dartmouth professors. Before they were eventually convicted, this article described them as being seen as "regular guys." Residents of their Vermont town were quoted saying, "There was nothing that would lead one to believe that they could do the crime they are accused of." In characterizing one of the boys a resident said, "Whatever he did, there was a reason for it....He's really smart, very logical" (Associated Press, 2001: A3).

We discussed how the cultural logic of ethnic hierarchies of intellectuality where white-skinned people were seen as superior to people of color was as prevalent in scholarly works as it was in the media. One example we assessed that had just been published at the time of our meetings was Hoberman's (1997) book entitled *Darwin's Athletes*. Although he correctly indicated that the Darwinian "law of compensation" was unfounded in its claim that the more physically gifted an individual is, the less intellectually endowed that person is, key aspects of his book ironically worked to support a logic of ethnic hierachies. For instance, he essentialized blacks as a group and repeatedly made unsupported claims about the disregard they have for education and scholarship. He also diminished the significance of genuine black sport heroes from Joe Louis to Jackie Robinson to Muhammad Ali and engaged in a form of racial name calling regarding the work of black scholars that he cited by adding the prefix "black" to almost every reference to their discipline and their work when this was not done with the citation of work and acknowledgment of disciplines of other scholars. The cover of the book had been shot in a way that showed distorted appendages of a black body in the pose of a caged animal, essentially swinging from a pole.

Subtle and overt ways that racial differences are portrayed in so many instances contribute to the stereotyping and denigration of blacks and other people of color in society and its institutional settings, and they continue the support of ethnic hierarchies of intellectual and moral superiority. They are part of the structure for policing the boundaries of perception regarding the kinds of attributes that attend to one group versus another such that even similar experiences [like applying to a school that does not require the SAT] can be charged with very different racial meanings. The complex play of race in American society needs to be looked at critically, and sport may be one of the more viable spaces in which to do so.

Aspects of Derek's positioning in the group offered participants alternative ways to consider how athletics and academics could be connected. One participant talked metaphorically about never being able to make the kinds of plays in the classroom that he could make on the field. Ernest added that it was the persona of the athlete itself that separated him in the intellectual environment of the classroom while being physically present in the space. "And that's why Derek's statement was so odd to me" he said. "I had never encountered anything like what he described as his experiences. I never knew an athlete who could say the things he was saying—making the critiques he was making as an athlete." Coming from an affluent background, Derek had described very different ways that his participation in sport was responded to those social contexts. He had talked about how those around him considered his sports participation, even as a professional soccer player, as a prolonging of adolescence. They always expected him to eventually "get serious" and resume his schooling and enter a "real" profession.

In contrast, when Malo decided to stop playing, many of his peers and particularly his former coach were extremely disappointed. They had seen a professional sport career as a paramount achievement and also as a way out of what they considered as undesirable conditions in their lives. There were limited perceptions of other professions potentially offering equal or greater fulfillment and achievement. It's revealing that the *Out of Bounds* participants were critical of seeing sport as a way out. Despite talking about being bound by the protocols and the paradigms inside the sport, of being shackled in sport, escaping those boundaries was a different proposition from the way that many youth had come to see sport as a way out.

Ernest made the following observation in this regard. "Once you get out, you realize that there is no place to go to—neither forward nor backwards. Athletes really do become alienated, they talk about your life is over when you're 21, when your knee blows out. You have no place to go, because you have been given an intentionally misleading set of facts about what constitutes success. That's why I really don't like that metaphor and I see it as a danger to view sports as 'a way out.' You follow the illusion of trying to make it out. This is something that has really plagued my young adult life. I went out and there was nothing out there. But then when I tried to turn around and go back, I realized there was nothing there either. So I was nowhere. You talk about space; there is no person in outer space like a former athlete with no other options. Everything you've been taught is like 'run through that door at top speed and then everything's going to be fine.' And you get through the door and everything's dark, and the person behind you is shoving through, and the way out is into the abyss."

"There's got to be more, Tony added. "People are hurting, they have the sport experience, but there's got to be a way to make it more full." "And if you return to your community," another participant responded, "it's always because you failed. If you do win and you do succeed you don't come back. The sign of victory is that you don't ever have to return. And if you do return, it is always, 'What's wrong with you'"? "I think that's the reason why my coach was so furious when I went back home, and he found out that I wasn't playing baseball," Malo continued. "He just felt like I had let him down, cut the cord. There was now no reason for him to be concerned about me. I'll never forget that look on his face. He just looked so confused and frustrated, and I was telling him I love school so much more. But it was more about him living through me."

Throughout these dialogues, the participants talked intently about how sporting practices impacted a crucial time in their youth when they were developing identities and their sense of masculinity. They recognized that sport did or could have important positive aspects that needed to be accentuated, but they also talked about the circumstances that eventually allowed them to make a critical turn from sport to a more dedicated pursuit of academic achievement. And, they all created lives after sport that went counter to traditional sport trajectories. The remaining sections of this chapter address connections between "sport and self" that occur during critical periods of personal development as well as considerations of some of the "positive possibilities of sport." It also discusses the contexts for "the turn" away from sports that was made by Ernest and Malo. Finally, it describes a bit more of the things they have accomplished in "after lives" beyond sport.

Sport and Self

For different reasons, Ernest and Malo found their desires to develop academic selves constrained by their participation in sport. Ernest had talked about not feeling safe in any other persona than that of a hard-core athlete, even while in class because his "entire image was centered on athletic accomplishments." Although he initially enjoyed that image, he also never felt supported by his coaches or teachers to develop a non-athletic identity. Malo had similar feelings of not being supported, particularly regarding his coaches who were interested in his development as an outstanding athlete only, no matter how hard he tried to be viewed and accepted as an excellent student also. Ernest's primary identification with his athletic persona was partially consistent with Adler and Adler's (1991) description of "role engulfment," the immersion into an athletic role while becoming detached academically. Except Ernest never really subverted his academic role as evidenced by his exemplary achievements. Malo seemed to resist the confining shackles of a sole identification with athletics every step of the way.

Both men began to distinguish themselves as athletes in middle school when they were in early adolescence, a time when boys are particularly susceptible to the influences of sport on constructing and defining identity and masculinity. A transitional time between late childhood and the beginning of adulthood, adolescence is a period of development and consolidation of one's social self—the identity and understanding of the self in relation to the social world. It is characterized by increased complexity of social behavior and group interactions (Lerner and Steinberg, 2004), and it marks the beginning of sexual maturity in terms of puberty and other aspects of bodily development. It is a time when the brain is subject to considerable structural development also where the regions of social cognition are implicated as seen from MRI studies (Choudhury, Blakemore, & Charman, 2006). Adolescence can be divided into three approximate levels—early adolescence (seventh grade), middle adolescence (ninth grade), and late adolescence (11th grade)—with the differentiation of role-related selves and tendencies to report levels of self-worth beginning in the early adolescence stage. Adolescents become progressively self-conscious and concerned with other people's opinions as they go through these developmental levels. Harter (1999) found that during adolescence there is a proliferation of multiple selves across multiple roles through which young people in this stage "become very sensitive to the potentially different opinions and standards of the significant others in each context" (65).

For young boys in the context of sport, those significant others are primarily coaches, fellow players, and iconic professional athletes; and their perspectives and practices have tremendous influence on adolescent athletes at a time when they are both susceptible and vulnerable. The coaches of Ernest and Malo attempted to exact a total commitment to sport identities that required them as adolescents to see themselves as athletes first and foremost. Ernest noted that for a while the intense commitment to sport created a safe space. All of his coaches with the exception of one were black as well as most of his teammates at the pre-college levels. "When I was in the gym, when I was on the field, no one could touch me; it was fun," he noted. "But it was the inability, and the more I think about it the more I hold my coach accountable, it was the inability of someone who mattered to me to show me that spatial comfort that I had as an athlete could transfer elsewhere, could transfer into the classroom, could transfer into everything that I did. No one really made that connection for me." For Malo, the influence of exploitive coaches, who could not see anything beyond the "dumb jock stereotype" as an identity for him, was mitigated by the influence of his mother who helped him see other roles for himself, particularly academic ones.

Because of the preoccupation with what significant others think of one's self, the influences from coaches, teachers, family members, friends, peers, and athletic stars are magnified during adolescence. These influences have impacts on the development of the self even when the influences are not understood or acknowledged by the individual. With increasing age an individual's self-concept becomes more abstract and less concrete (Montemayor & Eisen, 1977). From their review of developmental literature, Garcia, Hart, and Johnson-Ray (1997) noted "that the sense of self is composed of several forms of self-awareness and several types of self-understanding" (366). For adolescents self-awareness includes increases in self-focus as well as self-identification. Studies have found, for instance, that self-focus increased between ages 11 and 18 (Lapsley et al., 1986; Rosenberg, 1979), and it was linked to managing many stressful transitions including rapidly changing bodies, gendered differentiations, and the onset of romantic interests. All this is accompanied by stressors on and changes in self-identification. Self-understanding for adolescents is linked to ways that various qualities of the self receive social acceptance (Damon & Hart, 1998). The increasing self-awareness and self-understanding of adolescents also work to integrate gender identity and ethnic/racial identity into emerging, fundamental self-concepts, and these too are mediated by influences and social acceptance from significant others.

So, in the midst of forming athletic and academic identities, Ernest and Malo were also experiencing myriad forces and influences during adolescence on the development of their general self-concepts. They were vulnerable in part because of the overall stressfulness of this period in the lives of adolescents, but also because sport through its complex culture and practices directly engaged such fundamental aspects of their developing self-concepts as athletes, as students, as young men, and as racialized subjects. Sport influenced their development as men, but the influences had critical twists for them as black men in terms of the social categories that were available for identity connections. In part, this culture of sport had often worked to make them feel inadequate academically, or that academics were not significant in the larger scheme of things. For instance, it was only later in life that Ernest began to wonder why he had never considered himself a scholar despite his exceptional academic achievements throughout school. Sport practices often took advantage of their adolescent naiveté, insecurities, and ambivalences as these men developed self-concepts around masculinity, racial identity, and other personal attributes and sought guidance and validation through the social acceptance of significant others like their coaches and peers. As Ernest said, "I had my confidence coached out of me."

In analyzing the structure of the adolescent self-concept, Byrne and Shavelson (1986) delineated how it is both multi-dimensional and hierarchical. Most importantly for our purposes, they demonstrated how a person's general self-concept could be distinguished from academic performance. In their hierarchical structure, a "general" self-concept is at the apex, and it is composed of one's perceptions of self derived from interactions with significant others and overall aspects of the social environment along with self-attributions. Below this general self-concept are sub-areas of the self like one's concept of achievement in academic subjects and one's non-academic self. The non-academic self includes things like physical ability, physical appearance, and interactions and relationships with significant others like parents, peers, and coaches. Significantly, this non-academic self is able to be differentiated from other psychological constructs, such as academic achievement.

The ability to separate a non-academic sport identity from an academic self may explain why Ernest was able to comfortably reside (and perhaps hide) in his athletic persona throughout middle and high school and most of college as a primary identification fueled by powerful social influences and rewards from coaches as well as members of his teams, his family, and his community. Thinking back on the pervasive influences on him as a young athlete, he questioned if it was really feasible to identify with academics with anything near the identification that was demanded and rewarded for athletics. "Which would you have chosen?" he had asked the group regarding being in the position where both seemingly exclusive domains of identification were open.

The extensive sporting practices that work to shape athletic self-concepts and identifications in youth are influential in part because their impacts are not easily seen or understood during the vulnerable stages of adolescence, and for most athletes this also carries over into adulthood. Ernest was in college before he began to formulate a critique of how he had been subjected to these influences on his identity and his concept of self. Malo noted that is was not until the *Out of Bounds* discussions that he was able to go back and reassess the nature and meanings of his sport experiences. Clearly, it is not just sport, but the larger culture also that conspires to instantiate and reinforce a non-critical perspective in all of us, yet adolescence is a time of particular susceptibility. Opportunities to observe and engage in critical discourse are rare, and inside the space of sport, they are largely not allowed. The structures and practices of sport thrive on a kind of taxation without representation that ultimately does not serve important needs of the individual athlete and the broader needs of society. It's taxation of the physical body without representation of the needs of the mind.

Positive Possibilities of Sport

Despite the anger and resentment revealed by participants in the *Out of Bounds* group about their experiences in sport, they also indicated a number of ways that sport could have positive effects for individuals, schools, and society. Even though they villainized athletics at times, they also recognized its value. When they talked about how some people saw sport as a way out of undesirable conditions, they also saw other considerations for positive possibilities of sport. Rather than a way out, they discussed how sport could also be conceived as "a way back," where athletes could be the ones to exemplify a critical new synthesis of participation and performance in many domains of life instead of being seen as reflecting tired and worn dichotomies. As Ernest noted, "we can be the ones going back and instructing people to what sports can be."

We noted in the introductory chapter that a number of studies had attempted to examine the relationships between sport participation and academic performance, but their findings were mixed. While some reported that sport participation conflicted with academic performance, others found that the former actually enhanced the latter. In shedding light on this issue, we have foregrounded the stories and experiences of athletes who have consciously attempted to find balance in these separate arenas and who all ended up in rigorous graduate programs at the same university. Despite the mixed results of various research findings, we can say with certainty how well athletes do in their undergraduate academic subjects at Berkeley because it published these records by individual sport, by gender, and with comparisons to other undergraduate students at the university who are not athletes.

The "Student-Athlete Performance Summary" for the Fall of 2008 provided a number of interesting insights regarding the achievement of athletes at Berkeley. First, men's football and basketball—the high profile, high revenue-generating sports with the highest number of black athletes (with the exception of track and field), were the two sports of the 13 listed whose athletes had the lowest GPAs. Women's basketball was the second lowest of 14 women's sports listed, higher only than softball. The Summary also listed the historical averages for each sport, and in the cases of men's football and basketball as well as women's basketball, the 2008 averages were lower than the historical averages indicating that no significant improvements were being made over time.

Of the eight sports that had both men's and women's teams, women had higher GPAs in six of the eight with the exceptions being tennis and golf. Female athletes had 62.1% of their group earning GPAs of 3.0 or higher (with 3.0 or higher averages in 11 of the 14 sports listed), while 40.1% of male athletes earned a 3.0 or higher (with 3.0 or higher averages in five of the 13 sports listed). In fact, the overall average GPA for females at 3.08 was slightly above 3.0, yet the overall average GPA for all undergraduate females was significantly higher at 3.305. Similarly, the overall GPA for male athletes of 2.854 was significantly lower than the overall GPA for all undergraduate males at 3.23. Interestingly, men's tennis with the highest GPA of any men's sport at 3.194 and women's field hockey with the highest GPA of any women's sport at 3.198 were both still below the average GPA of 3.27 for all undergraduates.

In summary, women athletes at Berkeley on average get significantly better grades than men athletes, yet they do not do as well on average as women specifically or as undergraduates generally at the university. Similarly, men athletes do not do as well on average as men generally at the university. So, all athletes do not do as well on average academically as the university's general student population. Finally, the high profile sports of men's football and basketball that have the highest numbers of athletes of color have the lowest academic averages of all sports, and their average GPAs are far below those of the overall male students specifically or the combined general student population. Although this data clearly indicates that athletes at Berkeley are not achieving academically on par with other undergraduates at the university, there are additional ways that sport may be seen to have positive effects for athletes beyond their specific GPAs.

A limited beginning for some of the positives aspects of sport is in the perceived utility of sporting practices for engaging in other arenas of life. Ernest, for example, talked about how his coaches had continually made analogies between sports and life with the primary message being that sport can be seen as a training ground for life—that "if you can be successful in athletics then you will be ready to handle whatever life throws at you....You will be able to conquer the opponents that life presents." As an alternative to ways that sport is most often perceived, we saw some value in the promotion of these analogies through the lives of sport heroes who became prominent in other areas of life. One example that was in the media during the period of our meetings was that of Jesse "The Body" Ventura, the former professional wrestler and U.S. Navy Seal who said that he also wanted to be known for his mind. In 1998 he was elected as the 38th governor of Minnesota and served until 2003.

Another example that we read about and discussed was Kenneth Chenault who became the first African American to run a Fortune 500 company. In 1997, he was the heir apparent to become the president and chief operating officer of American Express that ranked 65th on the Fortune 500 list and had 70,000 employees. He had formerly been a top-notch athlete and graduated from high school as the president of his class, an honor student, and the captain of the basketball, soccer, and track teams. Chenault felt that sport did not necessarily make him a better person, but that it did make him a better competitor in life. In an article in *Ebony* magazine, he discussed how his success in business was linked to sporting perspectives. "You analyze the opposing team, the plays, the moves. What are the rules of the game, the weaknesses that can be exploited, and the strengths that need to be dealt with" (September, 1997: 59)? Instead of it being the quarterback metaphor that was crucial, he felt that it was more the coach "who has to understand the capabilities of the different members of the team, to inspire, to instill hope. The coach is accountable for the performance of the team" (59).

One participant echoed Chenault's perspective by talking about how he utilized a sport-like approach in his teaching. "I was so much an athlete that everything I did I had to do like an athlete," he said. "I teach like an athlete, like I'm in competition, and I have to be the best teacher. It's almost like it happened to me naturally....I think that sport can offer that." They talked further about how athletics could be used to promote academic achievement as opposed to being separated from it. Jabari connected this point to a book entitled *Making the Grade* by Covington (1992) that outlined an approach to "serious games" as a pedagogical strategy and curriculum focus that brought in elements of competition to increase challenge and engagement in learning. "This also leads to seeing how some athletes can take the mentality of the game into other areas of their lives," Jabari said. He talked a bit about his book entitled *Shooting for Excellence: African American and Youth Culture in New Century Schools* (1998) where he put forth the metaphor of teacher as coach and student as player in the game of learning as a way to change the nature of the traditional teacher/student dynamic for learning in the classroom. "Then we get into the notion of 'the player,'" Derek said, "and depending on where you are and the circumstances, that can have a negative or positive connotation....Somebody who is seen as an athlete first and foremost may be criticized as 'playing' the system just to get by academically." This was addressed regarding Tony in the previous chapter.

Ernest brought a different twist to the play metaphor we were developing. "For us the rhetoric was always that sport is not a game, but work," he said. This point echoed the way Tony had talked about his participation in sport in the previous chapter. "It was wiser for me to spend one hour on homework and five hours on basketball, because then I may have a 2.0 but a scholarship to college. If I studied for five hours, I might get a 4.0 but still have no scholarship, and still be flat broke, and not be able to go to college. So sports were never conceived of as a game. It was work, and in many ways for us it was more significant than academics. Everybody that we knew that had gone to college had gone on an athletic scholarship."

There were other ways the participants felt that the workings of sport might be brought into play in school and society. Although it's a de-realized space, sport has certain qualities that could help transform other institutional spaces. For example, sport is seen as more of a meritocracy than other institutions. The criteria for excellence are well understood and realized in specular moments in which accomplishments occur in set time frames. In four quarters the game is over, and everyone knows the quality of each participant's performance. "Gratification for achievement is instant and public," Jabari noted, "and it's also more equitable as opposed to the classroom where if a teacher doesn't like you, your grade could suffer." Athletes can see things in process that others are not trained to see," Ernest added. "Really, it's a kind of critique. You're making critiques on the field, and off the field, and being able to take that and apply it to other avenues like academics that at least are more viable alternatives to put that energy and ability into."

The participants took the idea of analysis into a discussion of the need for a Freirean critique or solution, "changing the language that we use as athletes," Ernest said. "Those of us who know going back and giving young athletes the words so that they can envision ways to make their experiences work for them beyond sports." We talked about possibilities for education to empower students through critique in ways that athletes often felt empowered through performance. In the Freirean sense, this meant helping youth to develop the critical capacity to transform their reality by helping them become "subjects" who know and act instead of being "objects" who are known and acted upon. So, beyond the accumulation of information and the development of specific technical skills, learning should also be a process of becoming conscious of how one's personal and group experiences are situated within and constructed by particular power relationships and historical conditions, and being enabled to challenge and change inequitable relationships and conditions.

Interestingly, Ernest researched and wrote his doctoral dissertation as well as other publications afterwards on these very issues. Some of his work will be cited in the last section of this chapter on "after lives." There are also a number of recent studies whose findings support the importance of developing critical consciousness as a key factor in achievement and success for urban high school students. For example, working with a sample of 220 urban adolescents Diemer and Blustein (2005) indicated a statistically significant relationship between critical consciousness and progress in career development. Their results suggested that by maintaining a critical awareness of sociopolitical inequity and by informing their individual agency with a critical reading of opportunity structures, urban adolescents were advantaged in career development processes.

These considerations are directly applicable to the experiences of our men of color in the *Out of Bounds* group, who felt that developing a critical analysis and awareness helped them survive and eventually thrive in the realm of academics and in their lives beyond school. They saw the need for coaches and teachers to be enablers rather than inhibitors of this kind of personal and intellectual development. The inequities that they recounted as athletes and as men of color occurred throughout their schooling experiences and even into graduate school. For example, Ernest, Mojgan, and Clarence Phelps were in a foundational graduate class on Theoretical Perspectives in the Study of Literacy that was taught by Jabari. They were three of only four students of color in the class of more than 20. For a required group presentation in one of these three-hour classes, they brought students from the Oakland, California high school where Ernest was teaching English to be a part of the presentation. The object of the presentation was to demonstrate ways that literacy skills were not autonomous as some of the scholars we read had suggested but instead were prioritized and given significance by cultural and political objectives and ideologies as suggested by other scholarly readings we had also discussed.

The high school students talked about ways that things they did in school were not often linked to their cultural backgrounds and interests, but how work they were doing in Ernest's classes built directly on their experiences and interests and helped them get excited about reading all kinds of literature including required canonical works. Ernest later co-authored an article with Jeff

Duncan-Andrade about this pedagogical approach entitled "What They Do Learn in School: Using Hip-hop as a Bridge to Canonical Poetry" (2004). When the high school students finished their presentation, the graduate students in the class were asked to answer 10 questions on a sheet of paper that would be difficult to get correct if one had not had experiences with hip-hop music and culture. The tension on the part of graduate students was visible and visceral, and soon a white male student broke the silence of the quiz by stating that he did not feel graduate students should be subjected to a test like this. A couple of other students voiced assent. The high school students were dismayed, and they talked about how this was the way they often felt when they were required to learn and be tested on certain things. The point was to give people who were studying for doctorates in education a sense of how students might feel while being subjected to traditional hierarchies of learning. Ernest, Mojgan, and Clarence tried to continue with the follow-up discussion they had planned on the considerations for teaching and learning that the demonstration had raised, but the emotions and anxieties of the graduate students had gotten so high that Jabari decided that the class should take its 10-minute break, and then return to finish the discussion.

During the break, a white female student asked to meet with Jabari in his office across the hall from the classroom. Beyond this particular class, she talked about the energy levels of discussions that had occurred in previous classes and how this conflicted with her sense of the kinds of discussions that should take place in a graduate class at Berkeley. Ultimately, she told him, she did not "feel safe" in the class. It was of interest in our discussions in the Out of Bounds group that Ernest had also noted not feeling safe in school. "I did not feel safe in any other persona than a hard core athlete even when in an academic class," he had said. This question of safety, the question of what styles of teaching and learning create safe spaces for which students, reveals key considerations for how schooling needs to change. As Ernest had to move beyond the boundaries and safety of his athletic identity to more fully engage schooling and other institutions in society, schooling also has to confront why its structures and cultures makes some students feel safe while alienating others. How can schools equitably engage students' minds as they are embodied in different sizes, colors, and gender orientations?

"People who are able to keep the mind and body together," Jabari noted, "have realized that the same way you figure out something on the court as a way of playing the game at a higher level, that playing the game of academics in the bounded space of the classroom at a higher level is almost like that same kind of move." One participant noted how he was never able to make those kinds of moves in the classroom. "I was always bound by rules in the classroom, you know write the essay like this, what is the correct way to do this math problem. And, maybe it's the classroom that makes this athletic/intellectual endeavor so difficult. The classroom is so rigid, and what we have learned as athletes is that it's not static, it's fluid, and we have to be able to play with the boundaries to be able to fully enjoy the game." "To come into the classroom and have that kind of a move requires understanding of the rules of that game," Jabari noted. "And that's where I think we often get lost with our young student-athletes. We teach them the rules of the physical game, but we don't teach them the rules of the intellectual game, and the fact that it *is* a kind of game that people are playing. They're playing with ideas, and they're playing with each other's minds, and there are all kinds of points being scored. And it's not just to reduce it to that, but to bring an analysis into play that allows you to benefit in the classroom as much as you benefit in the sport. It's about how we get kids to realize the game of the academy."

Ultimately, we discussed how it was more than just learning the rules and strategies of play in the academic arena—that also there was a pressing need for fundamental changes in structures and styles of participation in the academic game itself. When one participant had talked about the rigidity of the key structures in the classroom versus the fluid styles of key aspects of sport, he was actually addressing the centrality of the root-tree structure of hierarchical organization of teaching and learning that needs to be supplanted by a rhizomatic approach. We did not use the language of the rhizome at the time, but the conceptual framing for changes in approaches to education was consistent with that concept.

To transform the teaching/learning dynamic from one of teacher as the conduit through which all learning occurs in the classroom to one that positions the teacher more as a coach to facilitate students learning with and through each other represents a dramatically different approach to schooling. It makes the students themselves the primary players in the game of learning, and it requires teachers, like coaches, to build upon their individual backgrounds, skills, and talents and blend them in processes of fluid learning for the entire class. This kind of teacher would cultivate the multiple roots and shoots of individual learning and design experiences to facilitate the flourishing of these multiple entryways to knowledge and understanding. This approach would necessarily disrupt the privileging of hierachical systems of meaning making and transmission, and it would put students with their multiple entryways to learning rather than teachers as hierarchical conduits for learning at the center of the games of school.

The Turn

During junior year in college, both Malo and Ernest made decisive turns away from primary identification and structured participation in sports and toward more dedicated intellectual pursuits. All of the participants in the *Out of Bounds* group took note of these similar incidents in the stories of the two men. Derek connected these occurrences to Adler and Adler's (1991) book, *Backboards and Blackboards*. Their research found that during freshman year in college, athletes actually believe they are capable of becoming professionals in their sport. They usually continue to believe this during sophomore year. But in junior year, most begin to see that becoming a professional athlete might not happen, although some athletes never see or accept this. Those who do begin to change their focus. This characterization of why junior year is a critical time for changing perspectives about sport and one's future is a starting point for exploring the turn that Ernest and Malo made, but in the cases of both men, it was clearly more complicated.

In our discussions about Malo, everyone focused on the critical role his mother played in influencing his decisions, particularly in juxtaposition to exploitative coaches. Tony talked about how he was struck by the way Malo had depicted his mother's role in his personal statement—how she was described as the main influence in his life in his very first sentence, and how he described her complete support of his eventual decision to quit baseball during his junior year in college in the last sentence of his statement. Derek noted, "Anchoring the mother at the beginning and end of his personal statement revealed some of the social capital available to Malo, even though he was the first one in his family to attend college." His mother didn't only offer guidance on issues sur-rounding sport and school, she also made Malo watch the world news and talked with him about ways that minorities were treated in the U.S. and how black and brown people are subjugated around the world. These discussions helped him understand more about inequitable conditions and the kinds of resources needed to work effectively against them. Tony applauded the fact that Malo understood the commitment his mother made to him and that he was forth-right about acknowledging and personally thanking her for her support. "It's a testimony to his strength of character to praise his mother for never letting him doubt his own potential," Tony told the group. "Against this whole experience is the role of the male figures in Malo's life—largely absent, or when present, undervaluing the full scope of his hopes and dreams." His parents divorced before he was four years old, and afterwards he had no further contact with his

father. "With his mother's support," Tony continued, "his disaffection from organized sport could be seen as a 'rejection of the rejecter' that is addressed by
Bourdieu, and/or as an expression of his own desire to be free and not to feel
like a slave."

Malo responded to Tony's statement about him feeling free afterwards by
saying, "Honestly, when we started this project was the first time I actually went
back and reflected. To be able to go to office hours, or to go to a cafe and read,
to be able to go to the library in the afternoon and study, I wanted those things
so much that when I could finally do them, I didn't miss baseball." In Malo's
story the turn was predicated on much more than rejection of sport; it was fueled
by his intense desire for learning and to effect change in the world. He was one
of the few athletes in his high school who took honors and advanced placement
courses, and his love of academic pursuits was further evidenced by becoming
president of his school's National Honor Society. He was an inversion of the
typical transition from athlete to scholar. First and foremost, he was a scholar;
then, he chose to participate in sports.

Yet, Malo was so good in baseball that he had an opportunity to go professional and potentially play for the Toronto Blue Jays right out of high school.
He chose to go to college instead. He selected Berkeley because it was academically rigorous and because it also had a strong baseball team. But by junior
year, he found himself being spread too thin trying to be a student-athlete. He
felt his professors didn't really care about sports, and his coaches didn't care
about his grades as long as he stayed eligible to play. Also, he was angered by
what he saw as "unbelievable favoritism displayed on the field." It troubled him
that "there were so few agents, coaches, or scouts in baseball who were African
American, and that many of these people who had already gotten their education were telling me to put sports first." Additionally, he knew if he ever got
injured, he would be dropped out of the baseball program and forgotten about.
So, junior year was a turning point but not because Malo doubted that he was
capable of playing professionally. Instead, it was the time when he decided he
wanted to go to graduate school and, therefore, needed to be serious about his
academic preparation.

In solidifying the turn toward academics, Malo applied for and was accepted to a summer research internship at Brown University for the summer prior
to his senior year. This was a great introduction to the expectations for research
that he would eventually be doing in graduate school. He said that he had excellent faculty mentors in this internship who treated him like a graduate student
even though he was still an undergrad. They were also great teachers in their
disciplines, and they gave him lots of insights about the ins and outs of gradu-

ate school. In describing one of these faculty members, Malo said, "Listening to him talk about his research really made you believe that the world was your laboratory. He had a major impact on me." The program also gave him practical advice on how to plan for and apply to graduate school. It paid for him to take a GRE-prep course, and one of his mentors wrote a letter of recommendation to support his application. Finally, Malo noted, "The meetings with faculty and deans, hearing them say that you have what it takes to go to graduate school....It gave me the confidence and skills to know that I could make it."

"I like what Derek said about needing to decide what you're going to do by junior year, and for me it came down to a conflict with my class schedule and baseball practice," Malo told the group. He talked about how in the first two years students were taking prerequisites, and there were usually a number of them available to satisfy requirements. "Junior year is when students need to make decisions about their majors and start taking upper division classes," he said. "That's when you start juggling because a lot of classes for my major [sociology] were in the afternoon, and it was like you can't take that class, you got practice. I was about to not take a class when I realized why I really came to college. That's when I decided to quit playing baseball."

Like Malo, Ernest realized the pleasure and power of learning that was being sacrificed to sport when he had to decide on a major. "Selecting English as a major at the beginning of my junior year was the first truly academic decision I made for myself," he told the group. "With this decision, I admitted to myself that there was something I wanted to pursue in academics because I liked it. It also forced me to think of a future aside from athletics." He had a number of role models beginning with his parents who were both teachers, along with a few of his coaches and teachers in school, particularly his college English instructors. He was also influenced by a few motivational speakers and inspirational people that he met in college. Ultimately, he felt that majoring in literature and writing critical essays were pivotal to his turn toward intellectual pursuits. "I learned to become critical of my environment and to question things I have previously taken for granted," he said. He started to feel rewarded for his thinking as a literature major, and he had fond memories of being commended for his academic performances and treated like an intellectual by professors in the English Department at UC Santa Barbara. "I was actually asked to go out for coffee and to discuss literature, and all of this helped to make the transition to academia much easier." These experiences contrasted markedly with his earlier sense of isolation that had been connected to his former academic achievements.

Ernest's recollections about this period also revealed the development of

a racial and political consciousness in conjunction with his emerging intellectual confidence, and these were additional factors in his shift in identity toward
being a more critically aware and politically active person. Yet, Tony rooted
Ernest's turn also in the intensity of his conflicted identities. "The low expectations others had of Ernest's mind while they were praising his body fueled his
becoming....Out of his dual role as athlete and scholar grew a politicized black
man. A man whose transition to an academic identity followed the course of
radicalization." Ernest told the group that he was not really able to reflect on
the role athletics played in his life until he actually left the playing field. He
noted that there were three events that occurred later in college that turned
things around for him. In addition to becoming an English major, two other crucial events were the Affirmative Action debates and the L.A. Riots.

Affirmative Action debates reached a fevered pitch during the early 90s and
polarized many college campuses including UC Santa Barbara. Ernest saw that
many professors openly and candidly expressed their contempt for Affirmative
Action. He felt that all of the students of color were constantly under a micro-
scope, being judged to see their worthiness to be at the University of California.
This volatile situation resulted in his becoming very political while in undergraduate school. "I began to read more politicized literature. I attended rallies
and heard the likes of Jesse Jackson and former Black Panthers. I volunteered
to write for an underground magazine. I joined clubs." Ernest felt that all of
these things contributed to his forming a new identity outside of athletics.
During this same period, the Rodney King trial and subsequent L.A. insurrec-
tion occurred. "I was a junior in college, a burgeoning student, and attempting
to figure out what I wanted to do with my life," Ernest said. "This troubling
event forced me to look at my life and upbringing in a way I had not previously done." He talked further about how he had begun to understand both the
consequences of inaction and the potential power of the revolutionary mind.
He described events where he was wandering through the streets in the middle of the night, screaming at police and T.V. cameras. He joined a small club
that was able to ignite a demonstration that made national headlines, and
speakers from around the country came to hold forums and address the concerns
his group had raised. "I realized the importance of trying to be a catalyst in the
community," he said. "In a small way, I felt that I was part of something meaningful. The following fall, I applied to graduate school in education. I had finally come full circle."

The stories of Ernest and Malo are about ways they embodied and enacted intersecting and often conflicting identities of student, athlete, African
American male, team member, family member, community member, friend, and

peer. These were not simple, segmented identities, and they interacted dynamically to shape the changing perceptions, attitudes, beliefs, and values of these
men. They themselves were agentive at crucial times in the flow of their experiences in ways that allowed them to have or create choices and opportunities
in fields beyond athletics, but their acts of agency were always in the context
of particular kinds of influences. These influences were from individuals—
parents, coaches, teachers, community activists, and others; they were also from
large and small events that occurred in their lives—the public beating of a black
man and its aftermath, the political challenges to Affirmative Action, a chat
with mom about world events over dinner, a chat with a professor about world
literature over coffee. The point is that these influences affect change, yet the
influences of individual and institutional practices themselves can be changed
to provide the guidance and support needed to mind the body.

After Lives

Since the time when the *Out of Bounds* group began its reflections and dialogues, the arc of the participants' lives beyond sport has been more clearly
defined. Both Ernest and Malo have begun truly exceptional academic careers
even though both men are still in the early phases. As one indication of this,
Ernest completed a doctorate in education at Berkeley in 2001, and between
2004 and 2009 he has published five major academic books with a sixth book
under review in addition to numerous articles in peer-reviewed journals and
numerous book chapters. In 2007 he received early advancement to tenure as
an Associate Professor of Eucation at UCLA and has since become Division
Head for his division in the Graduate School of Education and Information
Studies, the Director of the Education Studies Minor, and the Associate
Director of the Institute of Democracy, Education, and Access (IDEA). Malo
completed a doctorate in urban and regional planning at MIT in 2006 and
became an assistant professor in the Department of City and Regional Planning
at Berkeley in 2007. By 2009 he had published eight articles in academic journals and was finishing his first book on the challenges that arise between large
medical complexes and adjacent communities around jobs, economic development, and access to health. This concluding section of this chapter portrays
aspects of their lives after sport to provide a sense of the possibilities that
many young people may have for personal and professional development.

Ernest received a Masters Degree in Language, Literacy, and Culture and
a secondary English teaching credential from Berkeley's Graduate School of
Education. While later completing a doctorate in the area of Language, Literacy,

and Culture at Berkeley, he also taught high school English in the nearby Oakland Public Schools. After he brought some of his students to present to the graduate class on theories of literacy in the school of education, Jabari asked to visit his high school classes to see his approach to teaching urban students. Oakland is an urban school district that historically has performed far below state and national standards for academic achievement although it has made modest gains in recent years. The district has about 40,000 students of which 70% are African American and Hispanic or Latino. Asians comprise 15% and whites are less than 7% of the student population in the district. At the end of the 2008 school year, the dropout rate was almost 40%. Interestingly, in May of 2009, Tony, one of the *Out of Bounds* participants, was selected to be the new superintendent of this school district just as the state was restoring its financial and curriculum decisions to local control. Jabari visited Ernest's classes on several occasions, and the following description is an example of what he repeatedly saw in terms of the intellectual complexity and engagement of Ernest's students around the literature and world issues being studied.

Students were in class well before the tardy bell rang working in small groups and discussing strategies for the trial that would soon commence. Ernest walked around to the various groups listening to their discussions as a few other students came in and joined their groups. The trial that had been going on in the class for a couple of days was adjudicating charges that had been brought against Geoffrey Chaucer—the poet, bureaucrat, and diplomat—best known for his widely read work, *The Canterbury Tales*. It is for *The Canterbury Tales*, in fact, that Chaucer was on trial. Some of the members of the group on the pilgrimage to Canterbury were extremely displeased with the way Mr. Chaucer had described or characterized them and their stories in his Prologue and in his *Tales*, and they had brought a libel suit against him.

The class had been organized into a prosecuting team and a defense team, and other members of the class had roles as the pilgrims on the road to Canterbury. Students also played the role of the judge, the sergeant at arms, and the jury for the trial. Key pilgrims were called to the witness stand in turn by both the prosecution and the defense teams to provide evidence for and against the claims in order to determine if the charge of libel and any punishment were justified. This called for the students to have an in-depth understanding of the description and character of each pilgrim as well as the range of stories that they told. The students took their roles and trial responsibilities seriously, and they poured over the text of *The Canterbury Tales* and debated strategies for the prosecution and the defense.

On this day in class, one of the witnesses called to the stand was The Wife of Bath. The defense team for Chaucer was relentless in challenging her claim that she had been unfairly characterized in the Prologue to the *Tales*. At one point one of the defense attorneys asked her directly, that wasn't it true, in fact, that she was a little deaf, and that didn't she, in fact, have big gaps between her teeth, and wasn't she really rather wide of girth, and hadn't she, indeed, had five husbands? The young woman playing the Wife of Bath thought about this for a moment and then responded that even if these things were true, who gave Chaucer the right to say and also publish these kinds of things about her? The discussion that ensued in the trial was intellectually rich, and it revealed close, critical readings of the text of *The Canterbury Tales* and imaginative arguments and connections to contemporary issues like intellectual property and the nature of literary rights and rites.

Essentially, Ernest was a dynamic, engaging teacher who designed instruction that motivated students who were seen by many of their other teachers as disaffected and underperforming to do rigorous, intellectual work, in this case around a canonical text. He continued to develop effective pedagogical strategies in working with these students and described the essence of this approach in the article co-authored with Jeff Duncan-Andrade entitled "What They Do Learn in School: Using Hip-hop as a Bridge to Canonical Poetry" (2004). Yet, years ago when Ernest responded to the interview question of why did he decide to get a doctorate degree he said that he felt he could do more to affect the quality of education for urban youth beyond being a committed, caring, and creative teacher. "I had had too much experience with what was wrong in public education, and I desired to find ways of improving conditions in our urban schools. Hiding behind four walls with 150 students a year wasn't, in my opinion, going to change much."

This was a remarkable statement because many would feel that being a highly effective, inspirational teacher of urban youth would be a major contribution in and of itself. And in truth, it is. But Ernest was also aware of the larger institutional forces that often worked to inhibit the kind of dynamic possibilities for learning that he was facilitating in his high school classroom. The administration in his school used to load his classes with what it felt were students with the worst discipline and achievement problems. When Ernest started showing spectacular results with these students, administrators and other teachers worked to constrain rather than support and applaud his efforts. So, getting a doctorate was part of his design to position himself to have a wider impact on urban schooling beyond the work of an individual teacher in his assigned classes. He wanted to research and conceptualize the most viable ways to transform both teaching and learning in order to ameliorate the lives and life changes of students who had been most marginalized in societal institutions and practices.

Ernest's dissertation research established the focus for an intellectual trajectory that has had major impacts on the fields of education and youth development. It was a study of the implementation of an educational intervention designed to facilitate high school students becoming critical researchers themselves as a primary mode of learning about the world and also engaging the world to make it more socially just. It won the Outstanding Dissertation Award from Berkeley's Graduate School of Education in 2001. He had multiple offers for positions in research universities upon graduation and began his career as an Assistant Professor at Michigan State University. In 2004 he published his first academic book entitled *Becoming a Critical Researcher: Literacy and Empowerment for Urban Youth*. He also published another book during the same year entitled *Linking Literacy and Popular Culture: Finding Connections for Lifelong Learning*. Influences from Paulo Freire and other social activist scholars on issues surrounding teaching and learning for social justice run through his scholarly work. In 2007, he published *Critical Literacy and Urban Youth: Pedagogies of Access, Dissent, and Liberation*, and in 2008 with co-author Jeff Duncan-Andrade he published *The Art of Critical Pedagogy: Possibilities for Moving from Theory to Practice in Urban Schools*. He published two additional books in 2009.

Importantly, the scholarship in Ernest's numerous publications has been highly acclaimed. His research and keynote presentations at universities and academic conferences like the American Educational Research Association have standing room only crowds of academics, many of whom are rising young scholars who have been conceptually informed and professionally inspired by Ernest's work. He is in the early phase of his career as a scholar who clearly will continue to do important work and have impressive achievements in the transformation of theories and practices of teaching and learning for more equitable and socially just outcomes.

Malo's dedication to social justice and transformational change parallels that of Ernest, and though he is at an earlier stage in his scholarly career, it follows the same striking trajectory. His experiences in a summer research internship at Brown were pivotal to getting into graduate school, and they also fueled his desire to use his professional life to help improve urban conditions and opportunities, particularly in the areas of health and employment. He was a member of the Housing, Community, and Economic Development research group at MIT, and his dissertation investigated the employment opportunities of urban residents within Boston's health care industry. After graduating, he was selected to be a Robert Wood Johnson Health and Society Scholar in residence at the University of Michigan. In that capacity he researched how race/ethnicity, socioeconomic status, neighborhood characteristics, and geography influence the health outcomes of urban populations. He also has an interest in understanding the role of new and emerging technologies and how they affect the work of health care professionals and the health outcomes of patients.

Malo had several offers for academic positions and chose to begin as an Assistant Professor in Berkeley's Department of City and Regional Planning. His current research includes an analysis of metropolitan fragmentation and racial residential segregation and its relationship to health. Specifically he is investigating how multiple political jurisdictions within a metropolitan region affect the distribution of resources across racial and class lines. He is also working on a national research project that examines the relationship between the built environment and health disparities, and he is completing a book that analyzes the role of hospitals and medical facilities as economic generators within central cities. In this book he discusses how challenges often arise between large medical complexes and adjacent communities around jobs, economic development, and access to healthcare.

Malo is frequently sought out as a consultant on sustainable urban development, and he has managed several large-scale research projects on this focus in both the U.S. and Canada. He has worked as an independent consultant for the Local Initiatives Support Corporation that is dedicated to helping nonprofit community development organizations transform distressed neighborhoods, and he has also consulted for NetFutures. He additionally worked as a research associate for PolicyLink, another research and advocacy organization that works for neighborhood development. He was also a senior policy analyst at Bosworth and Brian in Massachusetts, and currently he is a senior policy analyst at FutureWorks, an organization that supports the development and expansion of career opportunities.

Malo is dedicated to mentoring other young scholars in his field. "Now that I'm on the other side of the fence as a faculty member," he said recently, "when I talk to students, I walk them through the steps of what they need to know about graduate school and professional life." His research, policy development, and consulting work connecting health and economic development in urban areas might be seen as a powerful complement to Ernest's expansive work in education and the critical development of urban youth. As these two men have risen from sport, their contributions to creating a more equitable and just society have converged.

· 4 ·

GENDER GAMES

We have explored how sport is socially constructed as an intensely physical space, and an intensely masculine one as well. The stories of Tony, Derek, Ernest, and Malo illustrate a range of masculine subjectivities—Tony reading and writing to Emily Dickinson; Ernest engaging in political actions beyond the playing field; Malo realizing and acting on *real* reasons for going to school. Derek's story further showed how notions of gender and sexuality are far more variable than the rigidly ascribed categories of male and female, straight or gay. When girls and women enter the space of sport, their presence also complicates socially delineated boundaries and rules of the game. The experiences of Anne Gregory and Erin Conner Ngeno provided their own unique insights into ways that sport, schooling, and society engaged, engendered, and inhibited the development of athletes and scholars.

Anne and Erin received doctorates at Berkeley in 2005 and 2007, respectively. Anne's was from the School of Psychology, and Erin's was from the Graduate School of Education. Jabari chaired Erin's dissertation (as he did with Ernest and Tony). He was also a member of Anne's dissertation committee and the Principal Investigator (after Professor Pedro Noguera) of the university/public school collaborative that yielded the data for her research. These women were not yet in graduate school at the time of the initial meetings of the *Out of Bounds* group, and it was not until later that they learned what the group was attempting to do. As former scholarship athletes also, they volunteered to share their stories in conjunction with those of the men through many of the same vehicles that the men had used. These included several extended interviews, written responses to the same set of questions that the *Out of Bounds* group had originally generated, the writing of personal statements based on the same prompts the men were given, and the completion of demographic profiles. Using this data, we were able to bring their stories into dialogue with those of the male informants. We also brought their distinct stories into dialogue with each other—stories that revealed the play of gender, but also the play of race, sexual orientation, and social class in their experiences of sport and school. Both women were exemplary students, and they were also such good athletes that they frequently played with boys and men on otherwise all-male teams.

In some ways the "texts" of Erin and Anne's experiences were able to be read as chronotopic-like x-rays (Bakhtin, 1981) of structures and forces at work in the spaces of sport and school that brought issues of gender, race, sexual orientation, and class into sharp focus. Sport can be seen as an iteration of Pratt's (1992) notion of contact zones. But rather than colonial encounters, these women's encounters were with colonial-like mentalities regarding domination, subjugation, and sexualization of females particularly in zones of predominately male activity. Wilson (1994) noted the role of sport in reinforcing social identities and giving value to certain physical attributes by absorbing and reaffirming societal ideas about the body and the mind and the respective physical potential of men versus women, blacks versus whites, etc. Erin and Anne's forays into male- dominated sports revealed ways that dominant cultural mentalities about the place and play of strong bodies and minds were challenged to recognize new identities in these arenas—border identities as noted by Giroux (1994)—in this case tied to altering conceptions of how performance, power, and intellect can be embodied and displayed. So, these women's participation in sport with males constituted more than their physical presence and skills, it was also highly symbolic and a harbinger of the possibilities for changing dominant, colonial-like mentalities.

As Anne and Erin moved from the sidelines to the center of play, as they attempted to transform symbolic bodies into agentive ones, they experienced many destabilizing turns. They spoke of experiences and forces in sport and school that worked to segment and limit their identities with respect to gender, sexuality, and intellect. Their attempts to cohere identities as girls and later women who loved to challenge their bodies as much as their minds were often disrupted or cruelly contested by others whose own foundational identities were challenged by these women's intense competitiveness. This was highly explicit in male-dominated sport arenas, and the participation of these women was often precarious. As Anne reflected regarding playing on the boys soccer team in high school, "I felt like I was skating on this real thin ice trying to fit in. I was barely able to be in this space. And I felt like any move where I created rupture through my presence...they could just decide this isn't working. You can't be on this team. What were you thinking?" Yet it was precisely these precarious, courageous movements within and between the spaces of sport and school that revealed how societal institutions might be changed to better understand and appreciate the contributions of women and men as athletes and scholars.

Playing with Men

In 2004 Anne was awarded a highly competitive dissertation fellowship from the University of California's All Campus Consortium on Research for Diversity (UC ACCORD). On the return trip from the ACCORD conference that year, she talked with Jabari about experiences she had while traveling in Italy a few years earlier. Men in that country often wanted to bet money that they could beat her in pick-up games of soccer or basketball. It was like a scene from the movie *White Men Can't Jump* in which Wesley Snipes and Woody Harrelson's characters would set up bets with black schoolyard basketball players who thought they could win a game of two-on-two against them because one of them was white. For Anne, the misperceptions of ability were because she was female. A woman's presence on equal footing with men in physical domains often ignites displays of hyper-masculinity. The men would line up to play her one-on-one in basketball even though it was clear that some of them were not very good at the game. She always took their money. In soccer they would pair her for games of two-on-two with another player (usually a better male player to "compensate" for her being a female), and again she would take their money. "It was as if just by being a man they felt they would be able to win over any woman," she said. This is one of the ways that gender games are played that offers a chronotopic view of societal roles and rules in action. "I had a glimpse into this culture of the masculine," Anne noted, "this culture of manhood, of boyhood that was incredibly sexist and disturbing."

Erin's skills on the basketball court also allowed her to see and experience disturbing aspects of the culture of manhood. "Boys either won't play you, or they play you too hard because their ego is at stake. Or when you really play with them at their level, they get offended," she observed. To demonstrate her point, she described playing in a men's basketball league in which she was the only female player. Erin is from Riverside, California, and a tournament team she was on played a team from San Bernardino, California. She is 5'11" and the man she was guarding was about six feet with a muscular build. As he elevated for a shot at the top of the key, she made a dramatic block, sending the ball flying to half court. "It was 'all ball,' as they say," Erin recalled, "and the sideline started in on the oohs and aahs that were typical when a shot is blocked clean." Feeling publicly humiliated, the man threw a fit, yelling foul, and cursing Erin. When he didn't get the call, he started playing unnecessarily roughly with her for the rest of the game—shoving as she dribbled, bumping as she shot, and giving intimidating looks despite both her teammates and his telling him to cool off. "It was way beyond normal trash talking," Erin said. "He would make a shot and then have something mean to say directly to me whether I was guarding him or not." Her older brother, who had been a basketball MVP at Loma Linda High School, was not there that day, but he was livid when he found out what happened. His friend Kobe was there, and he had to check the man on his behavior several times. "I believe his reaction would have been much different if I had been male," she said. "He couldn't take the sniggering about getting his shot blocked by a woman, though I'm sure I was referred to as a 'girl.'" She appreciated the fact that the men on both teams had been supportive and noted that all guys don't play like that. Yet, she had experienced this before, and she had seen it happen to other women like her god sister, Princess. This time it left an indelible mark. "I didn't feel safe after that game," she said. "After that, I stopped playing with men altogether."

Summer (2003), who wrestled on boys' teams throughout high school, discussed some of the things at stake for men when women play sports with them on an equal footing. We will later discuss more of what is at stake for women too. Summer had been homeless for critical, extended periods of her life, but she ended up completing her undergraduate education at Harvard. Her experiences wrestling on all male teams as a young woman were insightful in conjunction with those of Erin and Anne. Like them, she had been one of Jabari's graduate students at Berkeley. There were times when boys on opposing teams would forfeit the match rather than wrestle her. In the first match where she was winning against a boy, he quit halfway through, saying he was hurt while grimacing and holding his side theatrically. Sometimes she would throw matches herself. "I would suddenly pause when placed in a position of power in a match," Summer wrote. "I later realized that I was afraid of how I would be thought of once I had proved myself as a competent wrestler. No longer would I be the cute little girl who tries really hard but is not a threat. I was scared that if I actually beat boys, they would begin to feel antagonistic toward me, a reminder of their inadequacy in proving their superior male strength. Instead

I was sometimes content with scoring a few good moves, improving, yet losing the match in the end" (192). On the other hand, the dilemma that boys faced in wrestling a girl was that winning offered no real proof of their skill or "manhood." Rather, they could come off just looking like a bully. "But to lose to a girl," Summer concluded, "would be an altogether worse fate, to be called a wimp and a loser and a weakling" (190).

Although it might seem nearly impossible for any of the participants to have a sense of winning when women play with men, both Erin and Anne received many personal benefits from their experiences in sport. However, the primacy of the male jock identity in influencing larger social constructions of male identities is problematic in how it is also defined in relation to the subordination of women and other groups. The very idea of "winning" in these dominating discourses needs to change both in sport and life. How would winning be different, how might it better serve society, if it were not predicated on various kinds of violence being inflicted on bodies and minds? How is this related to the kinds of violence that schools inflict on young bodies and minds? The stories of Erin and Anne provided important insights into these issues particularly as they are revealed in considerations and constructions of gender, race, and class in both domains. Their stories help us see directions that ameliorative changes may take.

Always an Athlete

Anne became an athlete much earlier in life than Erin, and like Ernest, Tony, and Derek she won an outstanding scholar/athlete award (in her case during senior year in high school). She was never really pushed to compete by her family or coaches; her intense motivation was entirely intrinsic. "Competitive movement, those feelings in the body, I was always happiest when moving and playing," Anne said. "I had been playing with boys as the only girl since kindergarten. So like at recess, for instance, when all the girls would be jumping rope, I would be the only girl, or one of two, playing football with the boys. Gym was my favorite class throughout school in the early years....Movement to me was a way of engagement that just felt freeing or natural or something. I was a very energetic kid, so after dinner every day, I would go out to the streets [of Brooklyn, New York] to play with kids. I was constantly looking for opportunities to get out and move and play."

Although she was never pushed into competitive sports, her brother, who was a couple of years older and her only sibling, played a pivotal role in her athletic development. From early childhood through adulthood, they continually played with and against each other informally as well as on a variety of teams. They set up the basement in their home as a private sport arena, and they played basketball, soccer, hockey, and even wrestled every chance they could get. "Actually, he and I would physically fight a lot, too," she said. "There was something about competition with him which kept me more engaged at getting better at the skills because I wanted to win; I wanted to beat him." The fact that he was older helped to accelerate her skill development, and eventually there were some sports at which she was clearly better. "Yeah, I was a much better basketball player than him," she recalled. "And, umm, ping-pong. So those were two things. But, neither of us would admit who was better. We would try dribbling around each other, scoring on each other. And never admit defeat—to this day!"

These experiences with her brother made it seem natural for Anne to play with boys and even to out-play boys without feeling odd or abnormal. Her father, a loan officer at a bank, contributed to her comfort in physical expression by not differentiating between her and her brother with respect to sport activities. He would go out and play catch with her when she was young, and he played basketball with her when she was older. He wasn't an avid parent/fan, however, and when she played soccer throughout high school he would attend about one game per season mainly to show support. Yet, he was always interested in what happened in her games, and when she got home in the evenings, he asked for play-by-play accounts.

Anne's mother, on the other hand, was always very nervous about her sport activities. She was a psychiatric nurse, and she also opened a private practice working with married couples and families. She was disturbed by the potential for injury and aghast at how violent things were on the field, but she didn't stop Anne from playing. She knew how determined her daughter was to be an athlete and to excel in sports. For example, when Anne was in fifth grade, she decided to play floor hockey in a local YMCA league. She was the only girl in the league, and she didn't even tell her parents she had joined the league. She got her dad to sign a check without knowing what it was for, and used it to pay the fee for the league. "I knew my mother wasn't going to want me to do it because she was scared for my physical safety," Anne said. She would sneak out early every morning to go and play, and sneak back in before breakfast, red-faced and sweaty. Initially, she played off their questions, but eventually she told them what she was up to. "You know, I joined this floor hockey league, and I'm in my fourth game. Do you want to come see"? Her mom came to one game, and watched from behind the door to the gym through a little safety-glass window. She was horrified by what she saw. She later told her daughter that she didn't want her playing these kinds of games, but also that she knew Anne had to do it. Still, she told Anne emphatically that she would never come to watch her play again.

Anne played softball, basketball, and soccer throughout high school at a private school in Brooklyn called Packer. Formerly, Packer had been an all-girls' school, but in recent decades it had become co-educational. Anne played on all-girls' softball and basketball teams, but she was the only girl on the boys' soccer team for the three years that she was in high school. Actually, she was the only female in the whole soccer league composed of about 15 teams. Packer had strong athletic teams and would often win division championships in each of the sports that Anne participated in. The school had a tracked academic system, and Anne was always in the higher tracks, taking lots of Advanced Placement (A.P.) classes during the time she was there. Even so, she did not find high school to be that challenging academically despite the amount of work she had in her classes. A.P. physics was an exception. "It was the first time I had really experienced what it meant to push myself and really be engaged in difficult material. So, for me that was the first experience I had with the struggles of learning and what it really takes to grapple with difficult material," she said. Her parents didn't push her to achieve academically, just as they hadn't pushed her into sports. They encouraged her to think deeply and critically about political and social issues with lively conversations around the dinner table. And, of course, they were pleased that she did well in school, but they were really hands off about it, and even told her at times that she might be spending too many hours on schoolwork. They usually found out what subjects she was taking on report card day. This was due in part to Anne feeling that her studies were kind of a private matter. She even objected to being named the school's scholar/athlete. "I had always felt like those aspects of my life were so distinct," she noted. "It was like one side of me not knowing the other side and almost like the school really not knowing either side. So to have that public recognition of these two aspects being honored felt good, but it also felt strange, like an invasion of my own private worlds coming together when I had purposely tried to keep them apart." Anne had compartmentalized herself into separate identities for academics and sports. It seemed intrusive to her when these worlds came together. She said, "It was like my different worlds were inspecting one another in a way that broke the unspoken rules about the rigid boundaries."

Making her academic accomplishments public was also upsetting because most of her friends were not on the honor roll, and most were not in her upper-tracked classes. "I didn't like that," she said. "I felt like it was private and that it also made other people feel bad. So I was always campaigning against that kind of stuff." She felt her friends were happy for her, but some were also a little jealous. She had friends that she would not see at all during her academic classes. Then she would leave them again to go play on various sport teams. Anne and most of her friends were living totally different realities in school, and she often felt a sense of betrayal by always leaving them to go play with the boys. There were times when this made her feel alienated, yet her friends were very supportive of her sport activities and would come to the games to cheer her on.

In high school Anne didn't necessarily consider her academic success as being very cool, whereas being involved and visible in sport was cool. As a team captain she had a daily role of getting up in front of a large audience of students and faculty and announcing upcoming games. "Just to have that leadership role, and to be so visible in the school was seen as being cool," she said. There were even some teachers who told her they came to games just to see her play. For example, she kept seeing her A.P. Calculus teacher at the soccer games. As Anne recalled, "It was very weird. She just doesn't seem like that type. And then one time she came over to me and said, 'I'm only coming to watch you because it inspires me that you're playing on this team.' I was taken aback, just to see my A.P. Calculus teacher at the game. Then, for her to say this to me. So, I feel like it enhanced some of my relationships with teachers because they felt like I was taking this step, kind of boundary crossing. And they were admiring that....Packer had been a women's school for a hundred years, and then more recently it became co-ed. So, I think it was something about the strength of women....You can be doing sports there and be honored in that, and be doing academics too. Somehow the acceptance of this was different from most schools. As a female, there was this element that that was the ultimate—to be able to do both of those things."

One of Anne's most memorable moments occurred during her senior year in high school. She was playing soccer in the championship game, and it was tied in the last 30 seconds. She took a long shot that hit the cross bar, and as it bounced off one of her teammates headed it in for the win. The fact that the kick wasn't technically considered an assist didn't bother her because she knew it had been critical to her school winning the soccer championship that year. Memories like this were tempered, however, by ones that were not so fond with respect to Anne's experiences in school-sponsored sport programs in both high school and college.

As noted earlier in this chapter, boys and men often responded aggressively to women like Anne and Erin with both physical and symbolic violence. The presence and acceptance of these features being embedded in sport and school-ing practices clearly need to be changed through efforts to create more produc-tive approaches to sport in high schools and colleges. This section reveals some of the insidious ways that boys, men, and women tried to push Anne to the sidelines of sporting activities because her very participation challenged the limits and viability of traditional cultural logics operating in these arenas along with the practices that supported them. Understanding the experiences of women like Anne and Erin in the varying "contact zones" of sport in schools is critical for re-thinking new possibilities for change because the nature of clashes between dominant and subjugated groups in these societal spaces illu-minates intricate ways that prevalent conceptions and practices can be nego-tiated and reformed. In other words these women's challenges to the boundaries and traditions of sport and schooling can be seen as motivating forces for ame-liorative change. We will address this with Anne primarily in connection with her experiences in sport while being an honor student, and later with Erin with more of a focus on her academic experiences while also being a gifted athlete.

"Git the Skirt"

Anne felt there were clear advantages for her overall development that were linked to playing on teams with boys and men. By being on the girls' softball and basketball teams as well as the boys' soccer team, she could see how the rigor of the training was incredibly disparate. "The expectations for performance and fitness were on another whole planet compared to my experience on girls' teams," she said. Consequently, she would have conflicts with the girls' team coaches because she would question how out of shape female players were allowed to be in comparison to males. "Whenever I was on a female team," she noted, "I would have to do a lot of training on my own to stay in the kind of shape I was in when playing with the boys." These disparities in athletic train-ing were mitigated when she played on the women's soccer team in college. And although she lauded the benefits of playing on boys' teams in high school, the intensity of her problems as a woman in these arenas may not have compen-sated for the advantages she experienced.

Males inflicted physical and symbolic violence on Anne in myriad ways both on and off the field. "Git the skirt" became a cover term for these forms of violence, but many male athletes on opposing teams used more sexist and offensive terms that were extremely derogatory ways of referring to the female body. Anne noted, "It was mostly they would call me tits. Or, you know, it would get into the pussy or cunt realm. And my hair, I had long blond hair. So, that was a given that I'd be called the blond. Git the blond. But usually if they went too far, one of my teammates would step up. A teammate wouldn't step up for something like skirt." Consequently, "git the skirt" was a term that was frequently used, but it clearly symbolized much more in these contexts, particularly since all the players wore soccer uniforms, and there were really no skirts on the field.

Verbal aggression was one of the ways players revealed that they really didn't want Anne in a space they felt was a province of men. It was revealed in many ways. Although the majority of players engaged her as a fellow competitor, there were instances when some of her own teammates were hesitant to pass her the ball. Some players on opposing teams would just let her maneuver the ball by them without attempting to defend her as if to show that her play was not worth their effort. These acts were upsetting and degrading and another downside to being female in a male domain. Additionally, as in the situation with Erin described earlier in this chapter, there were opponents who played incredibly aggressively against her and/or viciously insulted her. She tried to play down these situations, and she also got a lot of support from her teammates in dealing with overly aggressive opponents. Her brother played on the soccer team with her, and if needed she would tell him the number of a certain player who was giving her a hard time. He would thank her for telling him and confront the player on his behavior. Other players on her team would also step up in these situations. A teammate would overhear someone taunting her and just go off on him and demand that he not talk to her that way. Anne stated, "There was this whole other layer of complexity that I was grappling with when I was on the field, the taunts and all that kind of stuff. I guess I got kind of used to it on some level. And I would just screen it out, and really just focus on the play, and on my own performance, and about getting better. I mean there was this whole I'll show them motivation of yeah, I'm going to become a starter on this team, and watch, I'm going to dribble around you. And if I score, maybe you can't call me tits anymore."

There were times too when physical differences were heightened just through the way the game was played. "I guess it was like markers around my breasts," Anne said. "That was a big deal. And it would come up a lot during like chest traps and stuff like that. Because there was this whole idea that I had this impediment to play which really was not the case." She had vivid recollections of these moments when biological differences were accentuated because of some aspect of the sport. For example, when the team lined up to try and block a free kick, male players would position their hands to protect their crotches. But, for a woman, the logical place to protect with your hands was your chest. Situations like this presented heightened moments of choice for

Anne as she pictured how all of this looked from the sidelines. If she protected her chest, it further marked her difference, and if she protected herself the way the males did, it still looked weird somehow. Either way, these kinds of situations caused her to feel a sense of shame.

Anne's difference and denigration as a female athlete on a male team were reflected in many other ways. These difficult situations were not dealt with, or were just brushed off by players and coaches and school administrators. The team would play against all-boys' schools, for example, and there would be no facilities for her to change in. "It was very difficult," she said, "because they would try to make a space for me in the boys' locker room, and everyone would be laughing hysterically. So, while I was trying to blend in, I clearly wasn't blending in, and there should've been more adult support." In reflecting on these experiences, Anne suggested that there needs to more effective adult leadership by coaches and school administrators in developing school structures to support all types of differences in sport experiences.

We noted earlier how Anne felt that getting accepted in this masculine world was as precarious as skating on thin ice. Rather than this world expanding to accommodate her as a woman, her entry was more predicated on her assuming the status of an "honorary" male. She was accorded some of the privileges of male status but expected to adhere to an unspoken agreement to not use her acquired status to rupture or cause disturbances in the hierarchy of forces in this domain. Summer (2003) suggested that these ways of accommodating females amounted to a kind of tokenism. Regarding her wrestling on all-boys' teams, she stated, "People told me that is was all right that I wrestled, but other females were discouraged from trying it. My coach didn't really want his team to be taken over by girls who wanted to wrestle. Other girls were told not to try out because they were too sexual, they might be harassed. It was hard for me not to revel in being unique, to want to remain the only girl. Many women in positions usually reserved for men enjoy the glory and the power in being a token woman, not seeing that by allowing themselves to be perceived as 'the exception' they are preventing other women from succeeding" (192).

In her early years on the team, Anne's exceptional status was such that she was seen but not really expected to be heard. This put her in many compromising and embarrassing situations. For instance, when the team rode in the van on the way to league games, the males would talk about young women that she knew personally, some of whom were her friends. Team members would graphically discuss specific sexual activities or desires that they had for these women making no exception for Anne's presence. "It was so degrading and upsetting that I was exposed to that," Anne said. "I would go and tell my friends not to date certain people…like he's good, or don't date him because he talks terribly about women." But during these actual conversations in the van, she was silent. "I didn't feel that empowered, and I think I was in shock. I just I didn't even know what to say….I mean you can imagine these are like the hot, most popular, jockey guys. And they're coming together talking this way." Summer (2003) described nearly identical considerations to those of Anne with the only real difference being the sport she participated in. Regarding her positioning as an "honorary" male Summer wrote, "I knew that when with the wrestling team I ceased in some way to be a girl. This was liberating as well as crippling. It meant that I was part of a masculine space. It also meant that I learned to disdain femininity, that I had to 'be a man' because girls were weak" (191).

By the time Anne was in her senior year, however, she did begin to challenge sexist behavior by her team members. One other female had just joined the soccer team, and Anne felt that this girl was targeted and harassed much more than she herself had been. She saw it as her job to protect the new girl. During one indoor practice, four guys wolf-packed the girl as she was going for the ball and rammed her into a corner in a pretty brutal way. This wasn't called for in the game in any way. The girl was completely unsettled by the experience but tried to blow it off as if it wasn't gender related. Anne knew that it was, and she took each of the male players aside individually, outside of the gym and essentially went off on them. "I'm leaving this team and you need to respect her next year," she forcefully told them. It was the first time she had just let it all out. She knew how hard being on the boys' team had been for her, and she didn't want that to happen to another girl. Anne continued, "Yeah, and one person I talked to, I burst into tears throughout the whole thing because it was kind of like all my pain was surfacing."

Anne's personal relationships with males as a young woman were decidedly affected by her sport participation. She was comfortable around males, and early on she dated boys on her team. Sometimes she facilitated introductions between her teammates and her friends. Then, there started to be drama and difficulties playing soccer with males who were ex-boyfriends. So, she extracted herself from all of that by dating a guy who was outside of her school network, an athlete who attended a different school. She dated him through most of high school. "That was a good choice," she said. During the summer after she graduated from high school and was preparing to go to Brown University, something else happened. "I fell in love with a woman," Anne said. "That was pretty much it. I just kind of woke up one day and said, 'Oh my god, I'm in love with this person.' It's not you know, it's not about this person being a woman or not. It's about this person in particular. Just embracing that feeling. So that's how it all started. Although for a while, I was kind of, you know, feeling it was more bisexual." Was it also competition with men in another high-stakes field of play?

Playing on a highly competitive, Division One women's soccer team at a major academic institution like Brown was a dramatic change for Anne. "Suddenly I was no longer the odd ball worrying about the test or paper due the next day while changing after practice," she said. It was also very problematic and debilitating but in a starkly different way than playing on all-boys' soccer teams in high school. As someone who had just come out as a lesbian, she was conflicted by aspects of the culture surrounding women's soccer in this university setting. Yet, she was highly challenged by the level of academic work at the school and impressed by the level of academic engagement of her peers. This academic environment was exciting, and the intense quest she had for learning was pretty much the norm for students at Brown. "I hadn't experienced anything like this before," she said. "I would actually take courses based on the other peers who were going to take them. It wasn't just based on the professor. I knew the discussion groups would be interesting if certain people were in the class. So that was a big transition having peers that would push me intellectually." It was the first time that the rigor of her athletic training really interfered with her academic work.

At the same time, Anne was starting to see that she didn't quite fit in with the culture of the soccer team and its sorority-oriented social networks. The team's culture was linked to projections of femininity that were consistent with dominant cultural narratives regarding women's roles and physical presence. There was significant homophobia on the team, and if players were lesbians, they were closeted—passing for straight. The boys' locker rooms from her high school sport experiences were sites for displays of hyper-masculinity, and she found that the women's locker rooms of her university soccer team were sites for displays of hyper-femininity. For instance, everyone had posters of guys in their lockers. When asked if she put up a poster of a woman in her locker Anne responded, "My god, no. Are you kidding me? They would've tarred and feather me. No way." For a woman who had recently come out, the team's locker room was a difficult space to be in. There were some players who would not take a shower if a woman who was suspected being a lesbian was in there. Some women put on lots of make-up on game days to look more feminine while they played. They had drills in practice to try to get players to lose their focus and mess up while juggling the ball by teasing them with personal information like making public who a player slept with the previous night. But in Anne's case, this drill would completely break down, and no one would know what to say.

"Instead of, oh you slept with Mike last night…it would be this really awkward moment 'cause there was like no teasing that could occur around such a taboo subject," she said. "I felt there was a lot of hostility against being out even from some of the closeted lesbians on the team because it was like I was kind of breaking the code. Like we were not supposed to do this."

This code of silence regarding Anne's sexual orientation was an ironic twist to ways she had been silenced as a female on all-male teams. She had come out right after high school and was trying to get comfortable with her new identity. It quickly became clear that the team's particular culture of femininity was not a good match for her. There was a profound fear on the team of being seen as a lesbian or being too strong and muscular. Asserting heterosexuality was imperative. Consequently, Anne was extremely alienated by her athletic participation during her first year of college. Eventually, despite her love of the game, she gave up her soccer scholarship and quit the team.

Always a "Scholar"

If Anne had always considered herself to be an athlete while also being an exceptional student, Erin always considered herself to be a budding scholar even though she also became a gifted athlete. "Growing up, my primary identity was an academic one," Erin said. "I suppose I considered myself a scholar since the time I learned to read. I was three, and it seemed like such a big deal to everyone that I began to see it as my greatest asset." Erin came from one of those families where parents, siblings, aunts, uncles, cousins, and grandparents all would eat together at least once a week. These events would usually be on Saturday, or the Sabbath as it was called in her Seventh-day Adventist household, and they would take on the proportions of a Thanksgiving dinner. After eating, Erin's extended family would sit on couches and chairs around the living room while the kids came out one-by-one to do something that each was good at to entertain the group. Her brother and one of her cousins would show off their dancing skills with popular songs blaring in the background. Her older sister was specialized in acting and storytelling, and she would do things like Harriet Tubman monologues while in full costume. Others sang, played instruments, enacted skits, or did whatever they could to showcase their talents.

When Erin's turn came, she was always encouraged to showcase how smart she was. Her older sister and brother were just as smart as she was in her opinion, but as the youngest child in the family her love for learning was a special treat. "From the time I could talk in full sentences," she said," I was asked to stand in the middle of the circle and read a book or spell a challenging word.

I remember being in first grade and being asked, 'What is a simile? What is an idiom?' Knowing the meaning of these things didn't seem like anything special to me, until I was asked to regurgitate them as a magic trick of sorts. At six years old I was just excited about learning new things." She noted that these expectations from her family were probably the greatest influence on her developing an academic identity. Like in the case of Anne, Erin's parents also used dinner table conversations to ask the children their opinions on different things in the news or in their lives. This actually irritated Erin at times when she was a child, but her parents still do this with their children even though they are adults. One of Erin's artifacts from childhood was a little journal from the third grade in which she had to write "Thoughts for the Day." One of her entries was about how she wanted to get a Ph.D., and it was accompanied by a drawing of her holding a diploma. The academic achievement she is most fond of was being ranked number one in her biology class as a freshman in college. "I was in a honors biology class," she said, "and I wasn't sure how things would be in college with other competitive students. I have done things since that were more significant, but on a personal level that was the greatest feeling of accomplishment."

In addition to her family, the Seventh-day Adventist community that Erin grew up in highly valued education and creative talent. Children were expected to lead prayers, to help take up offerings, to sing in the choir, and even to preach the sermon on Youth Day in a church of about 1,000 people. Her first performance in front of the church was when she was four. In her church community, she had to memorize many Bible verses, play various musical instruments, and she also played sports. There was a gym attached to the church, reinforcing the idea that everything a person or family needed was within this religious community including schools.

Erin's family had always wanted her to be a good student and athlete, but it was her mother who was completely hands on regarding academics while her father was the one who involved her in sports. Her mother has a Master's degree in Education, and she has taught history and English in the Redlands school district for more than 30 years. Erin remembers her almost always going to school. For example, she went back to school at night and earned a law degree while working full time as a teacher, yet she never practiced law. She just wanted to know things. She encouraged Erin to become a lawyer because she was so good at debating issues. Her parents really wanted her to get multiple degrees—B.S., J.D., Ph.D. Although her siblings and most of her friends went to Adventist schools, her parents sent her to a small, mostly white private school in the Redlands named Valley Preparatory School from pre-kindergarten through fifth grade. Valley Prep was an excellent school academically with a challenging curriculum and high expectations for its students, but ultimately it had low expectations for Erin. Her experiences there were critical in continuing to shape her academic identity but also for the initiation of her identity as an activist.

The school's tuition almost broke Erin's family financially. Her father had to work two jobs and commute three hours a day, and her mother had to start teaching community college at night after teaching elementary school all day in order for Erin to attend this school. Consequently, she didn't see her parents very much and would often be at a relative's house after school or under her older brother's supervision. Her mother drove her to the Redlands every day to attend the school. Many of the students there were children of rich white people who lived in the hills, and the other students were from the Redlands valley area. As with Anne's schools, the classes at Valley Prep were tracked, but unlike Anne's experience, Erin's mother had to fight to get her in or keep her in the upper tracked classes. She remembers being the only African American student in the honors classes there. She had always tested extremely high on standardized tests. For example, on the Iowa Test of Basic Skills she scored in the top 1%. Yet, there were many stressful battles between her mother and her teachers around her being in the most challenging classes. In fourth and fifth grades they initially put her in regular classes despite her test scores, and her mother needed to strenuously advocate in order for the school to change her to honors classes. Some teachers treated Erin differently from the white students in class, screaming at her or sending her to the principal's office for minor things. "I didn't want to think it was racially motivated because I wanted to blend in, but eventually I realized that it was racially motivated," Erin said. "My mother would say have a good attitude, but as the only African American in all of my classes, I felt very isolated."

As Erin progressed through school, problems connected to having her academic talent accepted continued. One incident in middle school was particularly egregious. She was in an honors English class in seventh grade, and a substitute teacher was in charge of the class. She was a white woman who was around 30 years old. The substitute had given a grammar lesson on the previous day when Erin was absent, and she was giving a test on the lesson on the day that Erin returned. Erin asked if she could not take the test since she had been absent, but the teacher required her to take it anyway. She took the test and ended up getting an "A." As the teacher passed back the papers, she held Erin's up in front of the class and demonstratively put a big zero on it. She told her that this was done because Erin had cheated. Erin pointed out that she already knew the material on grammar, and also that none of the students around her had gotten everything correct as she had, so it would have been very difficult to cheat. But the teacher was adamant that she had cheated, and Erin was so hurt and angry that she burst into tears right there in class. Her mother insisted on a parent/teacher conference around this incident, and afterwards the teacher gave her a note of apology and admitted that she was wrong.

It was during this time that Erin was becoming more aware of the politics of race. She started reading a number of books like *The Autobiography of Malcolm X*, *Roots*, and *The Bluest Eye* and she saw movies like *Rosewood* that chronicled racial issues and politics. "I quickly found myself embracing black separatist perspectives and other militant views," she said. Her parents became concerned about her overall social development in the school she was in, and decided to transfer her to Sierra, a mostly black and Latino public school in the city of Riverside, California where the family lived. That move was key to what she felt was the best year of her life thus far. "I had black friends, so I did not feel like I was completely isolated from black people my age....I had the best eighth grade experience at that school," she said. Sierra had a black principal, Ms. Eloise Brooks. "She would single me out and protect me, Erin recalled. She also had never had a black teacher until she attended Sierra. "I used to sit and talk to Ms. Conway during lunch. All the black girls used to talk to her." Ms. Conway was a science teacher, and experiences in her class really motivated Erin to pursue science as her primary academic focus.

Erin's parents wanted her to go to an Adventist college, and there are hundreds of them all over the world. Oakwood College in Alabama, however, is a black school, and that is where she selected to go. She majored in biology, thinking initially that she wanted to be a dentist. She played basketball on the women's team at Oakwood and worked to balance the demands of sport with her science studies. "I studied all the time," she said. "When going to games, I would study on the bus and study when we got there. I think if I had had more of a social life it would have been more a conflict, but I was the person known as the one who was always either studying or practicing. I did both to the extreme. I didn't go anywhere on the weekend; I don't think I even went to a party during my first two years of college." But Erin realized during sophomore year that she didn't agree with the Adventist philosophy, and she also wanted an academic challenge beyond Oakwood. One problem was that her parents only wanted to support her going to an Adventist school, and it was a big deal when she decided to apply elsewhere. She felt that she could get into Stanford, but she knew she could not afford to pay for it. Also, Berkeley was the number one school in biology at that time. She applied and got in, but she had to support herself entirely. "I was a waitress; I was a tutor; I took modeling jobs on the weekends," she recalled. "I wanted to play basketball at Cal, but there was no way I could because to get through school, I had to work about 4 jobs."

"Give Me the Ball!"

Erin had literally been pushed into sports by her father, but she ended up loving to compete. At first, she strongly resisted even though her older sister and brother were accomplished athletes, but her father made her play. "I had grown a lot and thought I was clumsy," she said. "I was tripping over my own feet, and I also didn't want to ruin the family name." In middle school, she hit a growth spurt that left her taller than any of her peers, male or female. Her height was not a surprise to anyone. At 12 years old, she was 5'9", yet even when she reached 5'11", she was still the shortest child in her family. She recalled moving awkwardly with her newly acquired height and slumping when she walked. Her father decided that it was time she learned something else besides academic subjects. "Learning to dribble was excruciating," she said, yet basketball became her best sport. She also ran track. Her team competed well at the state level and brought home many awards. She played ball all through high school as well as her first two years at Oakwood, and she also ran cross-country in college during the off-season. In her senior year in high school she was captain of the girls' basketball team and was selected as its Most Valuable Player.

Like Anne, Erin often played with both her father and her older brother, but it was her father who was most responsible for her involvement with sport. He felt sport offered much more than physical development. For him it was about building psychological and emotional character and strength as well. Early on, Erin doubted her athletic potential and begged to be let off the hook and to not have to play. But, her father told her back in middle school that she would have to learn to play whether or not she was ever good at it because of what it would teach her about life. He banned her from playing with Barbie dolls when she was small (which she says she never missed). "He never wanted me to be a 'girlie girl' motivated solely by boys and having babies," she said. "He insisted that my sister and I play sports and play them hard." He went to all of their games, and cheered like crazy, but he was not into spoiling his daughters. He didn't want to know about Erin dating boys, and he was fine with her grades. Plus, her mom handled most of that. He was there for discipline in life and in the game.

Erin felt strong connections to her dad through sports. She was shy, especially around non-Adventists who usually seemed more aggressive to her, and she hated conflict of any kind. When she was first learning to play basketball, her dad took her to the courts on Sundays and showed her how to not be timid in the game. One thing he taught her was to at times yell "Ball! Ball! Give me the ball!" to other girls as she defended them. At first, this was difficult for Erin, but she eventually got so good at intimidation that a few times when she yelled "Give me the ball" at girls she was defending, they just handed the ball over to her. She also inherited her sister's court nickname, "Swat-sticka," for her shot-blocking skills. "I developed a whole new identity from playing sports," she said, "and some of that was good because I needed to be more assertive."

Some aspects of sport were also problematic for Erin too. She remembered her dad being proud of her capability to play on a level with men after having been such a timid girl at first. But the intense experience in the game with men that was described earlier soured her permanently on the game. "To this day," she noted, "I haven't played another full-court basketball game. I never really got over my hesitation to play with men, and there aren't many arenas for adult women to play together. I will play with my fiancé at the local gym from time to time, but it doesn't give me the same thrill as moving through a well-executed play in a full court game." She also noticed the disparity between support and resources for male versus female sports. "The men's team, whether high school or college, always got more things and better things. If we got t-shirts, they got sweatshirts. If we got sweatshirts, they got jackets. I asked my coach about that once. He responded that the men's team brought more attention to the school as a whole than the women's team did. He told me that when as many people came to our games as theirs, we would get jackets too." Essentially, she felt that the value placed on her participation in sport as a female was much less than it was for males.

Yet, Erin's sport participation still had tremendous value for her. She never depended on sport to get her other social advantages. It did not open any academic doors for her. Instead, the academic doors she passed through additionally revealed where she would next be engaged in sport. Ultimately, she felt she mainly played because she loved the game. But she noted that her dad was right about a number of things. He told her that it could help with academics through the strengthening of the will to run five miles or in other ways to push past physical boundaries. "I have never been called to have as much discipline and mental strength as I have when training with my team," Erin said. "I have never had to adjust every part of me, mentally, emotionally, and physically, as fluidly as I have had to while playing basketball. I have never been forced to immediately 'let it go,' whether disappointed with a missed shot or angry at referee, as often as I have while playing a high stakes game. I had to take another step when my body said I couldn't, climb another bleacher, run another mile, take another risky shot, over and over again." So, she did credit sport with being connected to her success in academics and in other areas of her life.

When Erin transferred to Berkeley in her junior year, she knew she had to give up basketball. She was accepted to Berkeley to major in biology, and she didn't want her grades to slip. It would be more challenging academically than Oakwood, and she wanted to face it full on. So, she never gave a second thought to leaving basketball behind, even though she would still miss it a lot. It had taught her some of the lessons that had motivated her to become a scholar at a place like Berkeley in the first place. "I learned to assert myself with confidence and ask for what I want. I learned how to get over disappointments. Most importantly, I learned to trust myself. Even when I missed the last shot, there was always the next game to look forward to." Although she does not play any organized sport as an adult, she still considers herself to be an athlete. "Not because I can run out there and hit ten three-pointers in a row, but because I took the time and energy to develop the mind of an athlete, and that is always with me," she said. "I am still working on having the athletic body to match. I still run, lift weights, and when I can, play ball. I wear my old high school and college gear proudly, and can't wait to teach my kids to yell 'BALL! Give me the ball!'"

Scholars and Activists

Participation in sport helped Erin and Anne as well as the male informants become more aware and more active in social issues in and beyond their varied academic settings. Anne traced her social activism back to tenth grade in high school when she was doing a lot of reading and thinking about the forces in society and how conditions could be made more equitable. She had started studying about labor and resistance movements and began imagining what her sense of utopia would be in conjunction with how academics could be connected. She had high school teachers who helped her realize that these issues were important scholarly pursuits. She came to see through her experiences in sport that inequitable gender practices were key to and reflective of other inequitable and marginalizing practices within schools and society. When she quit the soccer team at Brown, she joined an outreach group that was working on these issues, and she eventually formed a new outreach group that offered to lead panels and discussions for every team on issues like sport and gender and sexuality. These panels opened discussion around what it is like to be a physically strong women and to be straight or gay. They probed why it was threatening to some women to have strong muscles and other ways that women were grappling with the female form. These discussions quickly tapped into tensions around sexual orientation in terms of how it was expressed, how it was accepted, how it was camouflaged.

A lot of teams refused to let Anne's group talk to them. They did a panel with her former soccer team, and things pretty much exploded. The attempt at facilitation broke down as sides were drawn, and there were also lots of tears. "I can't tell you how cautious it was," Anne noted. "They wouldn't really quite come out and talk about things that everyone was feeling. And the coaches' perspective was that if we talk about this issue, it's too divisive. We can't talk about homophobia on this team because it will shatter us. And so instead, we're going to pretend everything's fine....There are similar issues around race, but we can't talk about them." A lot of coaches would not let Anne's group even present to their teams, but the issues did not go away. On the soccer team, for example, not long after Anne quit, ten other players quit. The team lost a number of starters and was effectively decimated. "And, it was all connected to these tensions," Anne said.

In conjunction with her activism, Anne's scholarship in college, in graduate school, and as an Assistant Professor of School Psychology has directly focused on social justice issues. Her dissertation that she and Rhona Weinstein published in the *Journal of School Psychology* is entitled "The Discipline Gap and African Americans: Defiance or Cooperation in the High School Classroom" (2008). In this work, she used a mixed-methods approach to understand and analyze the reasons and underlying dynamics of race and schooling that contribute to African Americans being highly over-represented in school suspensions. Understanding and effectively addressing these issues are important considerations in closing the racial achievement gap and in making academic access and success more equitable in U.S. schools. Her dissertation won the American Education Research Association, Division K Outstanding Doctoral Dissertation Award in 2006. This focus in her dissertation has framed her program of research and scholarship as an academic since being hired at the University of Virginia. In addition to systematic inquiry into identification of teacher practices and school policies that are linked to a reduced racial discipline gap, her work has expanded to include understanding the school-level protective factors and promising teacher interventions that reduce the referral of African American students for both disciplinary sanction and special education services. Anne has continually been an activist on social justice issues all during school and after working in areas like state prisons and on issues of gay and lesbian leadership in the professions.

Erin's continued focus on social justice issues began early in her schooling experiences, and as with Anne they also extended into other areas of her life beyond her school. Her heightened understanding and resistive responses to racial inequities began as early as middle school, and her mother played a key role in protecting and advocating for her throughout her K-12 schooling. Reactions to Anne's gender difference in all-male sport contexts had interesting parallels to Erin's racial difference in all-white school contexts. These racialized situations continued for Erin throughout grade school, college, and graduate school. One incident was written up in the *San Francisco Chronicle* in an article entitled "Everyday Indignities: The Banality of Bias" (Mahiri, Sept. 9, 2001). In this incident that occurred near the time of her completion of undergraduate school, she was almost arrested while working as an intern in a secure, high-tech science lab. Despite the fact that she was wearing her security badge and had worked in the lab for more than a year, a white administrator who didn't know her stopped her and questioned her and then called the police to have her removed from the building. He didn't believe that a young black woman could possibly be working at the lab legitimately. This incident echoed so many other experiences that Erin had had where her legitimacy was questioned whether it was for being able to pass a quiz without preparing for it or being accepted into upper track classes when she had scored in the 99th percentile. She survived these incidents because she had countervailing forces to support her from her parents and her Adventist community to her own will and determination forged through sport and other developmental experiences.

Despite having to work to support herself at times while completing undergraduate and graduate school, Erin was involved in numerous organizations and activities to transform the conditions of urban youth. She was a science instructor for a program call Black Academic Motivators, a mentor and tutor in the AVID program, a mentor for the I Have a Dream program, a youth counselor for director of development for a program called Leadership Excellence, and a college preparation workshop leader. She has been a board member of numerous youth development organizations like the Stiles Hall Mentorship Organization, the Kappa Achievement Fund, the Uhuru Education Program, the Hope Preparatory Academy, and Saving our Sisters/Saving Ourselves. She was a founder of the Black Graduate Student Association at Berkeley, and she also taught courses on "Race and Ethnicity inside Schools" to undergraduates there. She is an active member of the National Council of Negro Women.

Erin's research focus, like Anne's, addressed racial inequalities in schooling, but it looked at how these issues were reflected in images and ideologies at the intersection of language and electronic media rather than specific disciplining disparities. She co-wrote a research article that explored ways that black youth culture was positioned in the dominant discourse and media entitled "Black Youth Violence Has a Bad Rap" that appeared in the *Journal of Social Issues* (2003). Her dissertation that was completed in 2007 addressed these issues in more detail by showing how the pressure to assimilate into mainstream American culture plays out linguistically along with the educational and societal consequences for African American youth. She showed how African American youth who use African American Vernacular English are the targets of stereotypes and ridicule while simultaneously its use by non-blacks was often appropriated to serve the media and marketing interests of others.

African Americans are often seen to be perpetrators of violence, but the scholarship of Erin and Anne reveals how they are pervasively victimized by physical and symbolic violence through specific responses to their culture as it is expressed through language and behavior in school and in society. In addition to exposing ways that these racial and gender games are played, they have also worked to change the rules.

· 5 ·

NEW SPACE FOR SPORT
AND SCHOOL

The six performative narratives of intentionality revealed in the preceding chapters illuminate the unique struggles of four men and two women over time at the intersection of the cultural divide of sport and school, of mind and body. These border crossings were difficult, at times painful, as each sought out new alternatives and possibilities of self. Each of their stories of becoming provided an initial palette upon which other members of the group found pattern, color and lines of demarcation. In coming together to reflect on similar but distinctly different travels, the individuals came to understand their journeys more clearly. What these six individuals shared in their lived experiences focused on their complex, fluid and nuanced relationship connecting èlite academics and athletics. These relationships were complex because the intersecting spaces of schools and sports reveal the underlying depths of power and privilege, fear and alienation, access and expectation inherent to these spaces. The relationships were nuanced and fluid because each of these individuals were more than mere athletes seeking to become scholars, more than performative bodies disciplined and trained on playing fields and in the classroom. The six shared able bodies and a physical consciousness within the social geography of these spaces. They also shared the experience of stepping out of the prescribed boundaries of these spaces, revealing the very limitations of their movement.

Their emerging identities within social categories of class, race, gender and sexuality layered these experiences. The intersubjective analysis *of* these young men and women *by* these young men and women thickened the description of their lived experiences. The palettes were dirtied in the process, but somehow the process led to greater clarity for those involved. Each of these individuals likewise shared the experience of a turning point, or more accurately, a series of turning points, which led them to reject the institutionalized division separating school and sport while embodying a consciousness of mind and the creativity of scholarship. These unique but similar narratives reflect patterns of forces and understanding in and through the space of sport and school, offering implications for how we might re-conceive these social institutions, in isolation and in relationship to one another. There are implications for the social space of sports in American culture, implications for our educational system, and implications for the proper place of sport within our schools. The stories told within this book reflect the lived experiences of conflict and fracture but also freedom and creativity. These six men and women embodied the conflict inherent to these institutions or fields, struggling to reposition themselves on the playing field and in the classroom. Thus, the articulated experiences of a few, refracted through the perceptions of a few more, provide an opportunity to reflect on larger social issues within American sport and education. The following implications, then, offer the possibility to reconceptualize the relationship of sport and school and the ways in which youth struggle to be free to develop a sound mind in a sound body, or what the Roman poet Juvenal (10.356) articulated as *mens sana in corpore sano*.

Implications for Sport and Schools

In this final chapter, a number of implications for sport and schools will be made that draw upon the findings from the stories of the *Out of Bounds* participants. While these implications will be explicated more fully in the following pages, they are highlighted in this section. First, teachers, coaches, and administrators need to be more keenly aware of and able to accommodate diverse styles and needs for participation in classrooms and on playing fields. In part, this involves imagining and creating opportunities for more active and individually affirming approaches to teaching and learning. Clearly there is a need to "open the field of play" or in other words to actualize a more balanced approach to mind and body work. This approach suggests recognizing the intellectual discourse of sport and the physical nature of learning. Understanding and valuing a kinesthetic style of learning could prompt a similar somatic style of teaching in the classroom. In gymnasiums, sport and physical education need to be offered once again for all students and not merely the èlite, able-bodied athletes. There are many opportunities to learn within sport other than simply training a select few to win. For example, we might begin to highlight the roles of students assisting one another more than scoring above each other in creating a more positive and collaborative learning environment in both sport and school. A shift towards a safer, more open field of play requires that we not position youth in ways which limit their potential, put them at risk, and stifle opportunities for success. As a nation, we need to change the language and practices of sport and school to include rather than exclude, to redefine measures of success, and offer more rather than fewer opportunities for mobility and freedom.

Tony noted during one of the dialogic sessions of the *Out of Bounds* group that "there needs to be a radical reforming of how sport is framed in American culture." His experience with sport did not seem to be isolated in relation to the other members of the group. There was general agreement among the group that sport needed to be more fully critiqued and not simply accepted to function in society as a positive vehicle for racial and ethnic integration, social and economic mobility and personal development. Their lived experiences evidenced that such functional, acritical and ahistorical readings were fraught with danger.

On the surface, sport provides much to a society and its citizens. It unifies people, provides a way of coming together and collaborating around a common goal. Sport instills pride and discipline, building the character of those engaged in its rigorous physical and moral practices. Sport is an escape from reality, entertainment, fun. As Bourdieu has noted, however, the space of sports exists as a field within larger social structures, a universe independent but likewise contingent upon the reigning cultural ideology. The practitioners within this space, the athletes themselves, embody these structures.

Their bodies, both physically and socially, move upon these playing fields, producing a freedom and creativity of action while reproducing the dominant discourses that significantly limit their range of motion. These bodies both experience and represent pain and possibility, exploitation and liberation. Athletes are trained physically, to become stronger and faster and to master their competition. They must learn to read the game and their opponent, to become fluent in the literacy of physical competition. This somatic literacy, a kind of kinesthetic consciousness, relies heavily on reaction rather than reflection, impulse over contemplation. The successful athlete contextualizes the situation, recognizes patterns and themes and seeks out flaws in flow and consistency. Just as athletes and their bodies are read as texts, so too do athletes read the game and their active role within the game. That this form of literacy relies on fast-twitch muscles and spit-second decision-making does not make the reading of the game any less skillful. The process is active and analytical. But because this action is primarily physical, of the body, the strategic and purposeful analysis is somehow discounted intellectually. This is particularly the case when the space of sport is embedded within the social institution of school, where exercises of the mind are more valued than those of the body.

Thus, one implication for educators, teachers, coaches and administrators is to celebrate exercises of the mind in the field of sport and its possible transferability into the classroom. Fluency in any form of literacy demonstrates an ability to understand the syntax and structure of language. While teachers have learned to place greater emphasis on the existing cultural literacies of their students, recognizing that the social and cultural backgrounds and styles of learning of these young people matter, seldom do educators specifically acknowledge an athletic literacy. When they do, it is often seen as a hindrance rather than an advantage to developing an academic fluency. Because the body is more often disciplined in the classroom to be still, attentive, and controlled, most curriculum and pedagogy in schools separates a quiet body from an active mind.

But this apparently valid style of learning often relies on physical forms of understanding and experiencing the world. This "kinesthetic intelligence" generally refers to well-coordinated physical and motor skills and an aptitude for communicating with your body. Such somatic consciousness also presumes a well-developed physical memory. Acknowledged as common among architects, surgeons and sculptors, the well-developed body is most commonly associated with manual, menial labor and the province of athletes and sport. It is not surprising, therefore, that these forms of engagement are also associated with working class and black men, who are often seen to dominate these spaces. Rather than unconsciously devaluing this form of knowledge as low-brow and anti-intellectual, schools and teachers might try to incorporate such skills and understandings into learning about other fields and disciplines, as well as integrate this type of learning into the daily activities of the classroom.

Changing the Language of Sport

As aired at the 2007 Sports Industry Awards in London, Nelson Mandela is quoted as saying that "sport speaks a language which is understood by everyone in the world." As the preceding text has revealed, sport is also a language which structures a binary logic, separating winners and losers based upon a supposed true meritocracy. Imagine, for example, a foot race of ten individuals. The premise is that all begin at the starting line as equals, with equal opportunity to succeed. The spoils of sport will be rewarded to the true winner, regardless of social or economic position. Black or white, rich or poor, the meritocracy of sport will prevail, eradicating social inequality by offering a level playing field. It is within this narrative and logic that success stories and rags to riches tales demonstrate the historical and cultural glories of sport in society. There is some merit to this sport-as-meritocracy story, but there may also be a need to say a little more about this language of sport. For example, sport separates ability and disability, celebrating a physical and social elitism. One might argue that this is an intentional aspect of meritocracies, but it is not the case that all individuals have the same chance at winning.

Thus, another implication for sport organizations and educational institutions at all levels is to make the experience of physical education more available to the young people they serve rather than framing such education as simply sport, defined and experienced as the province of èlite athletes. This is particularly important as schools are eradicating their PE curriculum and doing away with extracurricular athletic activities for the general student body, based upon budgetary constraints. These decisions further separate the notion of physical education from sport, activities for all from the èlite activities of the few.

Our informants described the multiple benefits that each experienced in and through their embodied actions. Anne and Derek recalled the "pleasures" of bodily movement, the tactile and sensual euphoria of being at one with the body in motion. These actions were often personally challenging and internally motivating. These same emotions of motion can likewise be experienced by beginners as well as professionals, provided the proper space. Erin was pushed into these physical activities by her dad, and would not have done it without encouragement, but found both physical and social benefits (and that she had skills) once she opened herself to the experience. She was able to transition from physical education into more competitive sport with fluidity and encouragement. The challenge becomes how our educational institutions can facilitate more young people experiencing these benefits at varying levels.

Recalling the importance of physical education in schools may be even more pressing given the rise of childhood obesity, due in part at least to physical inactivity. Just as learning styles are varied and intelligence is no longer seen as fixed, there needs to be an educational refocusing placed upon both physical and intellectual development for all students, regardless of perceived ability. Rather than seeking out, recruiting and developing the highest performance of selected "èlite" athletes, educational institutions should draw out and draw upon the potential of all young people to sharpen and tone their developing minds and bodies.

This is not a revolutionary idea. At the turn of the twentieth century, American philosopher and educator John Dewey wrote in *The School and Society* (1900) that "what we want is to have the child come to school with a whole mind and a whole body, and to leave school with a fuller mind and an even healthier body" (97). Within his design of the ideal school, "the active life carried on its four corners brings with it constant physical education, while our gymnasium proper will deal with the particular weaknesses of children and their correction, and will attempt more consciously to build up the thoroughly sound body as the abode of the sound mind" (97–90). It is worthy of note that the entire school, circumscribed by its four corners, provided a space for physical education while the gymnasium served to strengthen existing weaknesses among children. The gymnasium today, as well as sports fields, are often reserved for well-trained, èlite athletes within the school and not for those seen as less able-bodied.

Despite the potential positive experiences of individuals engaged in physical education or sport, the *Out of Bounds* group recognized the limiting structure of sport as a social form of communication. As described in chapter three, Ernest called for changing the language of sport and "giving young athletes the words so that they can envision ways to make their experiences work for them beyond sports." This Freirean notion of critical pedagogy could be utilized in sporting communities, empowering individuals to feel and envision themselves as subjects rather than objects. This process of becoming conscious and critical was a central component for the members of the *Out of Bounds* group. Ernest saw this possibility for young athletes to turn the spotlight on themselves not for media attention but for self-reflection of one's own experience situated and constructed within particular power relationships and historical conditions. They could make critiques on and off the field and apply this practice of analysis to other areas and disciplines in their lives, in and out of school settings. From a larger social perspective, an implication for educators and social critics is to open up a wider dialogue about the ways in which the language of sport might better frame an understanding of race, social class, gender, and sexuality within American society.

Taking on a critical perspective of sport often did not occur for the informants until they were in college. Many years of being positioned as objects had passed and left their mark. For Ernest and Malo, both of these young men did not come to truly question themselves as bound athletes, enslaved by the mutually exclusive spaces of sport and school, until their junior year at the university. This was the same time that Derek opted to study abroad and forgo playing another season of soccer, despite his value to the team and the dismay of his coach and several teammates. It was an important turn towards academics and a scholarly identity.

During the summer following his junior year in college, Malo applied for and was accepted to participate in a research internship at Brown University, on the other side of the country. While there, he was taken seriously as an aspiring scholar, perhaps for the first time in his life. The experience allowed him to take pause and reflect on his athletic practice and the way in which he had long been positioned on the playing field. The young man had the potential for many things. He could have skipped college altogether to play professional baseball for the Toronto Blue Jays. He did not. He could have returned from his summer research internship and resume playing baseball with a good chance of being drafted once again to play professional ball. Once again, he did not. In fact, he quit baseball for good, a dramatic turn towards scholarship and the intellectual exercises of the mind. Malo's rejection of sport in favor of school, while powerfully symbolic, need not have occurred.

The very act of having to choose one practice over the other, an either-or proposition of school or sport, reveals the institutionalized conflict inherent within our schools and universities. The freedom Malo experienced in quitting baseball after his junior year highlighted the ways in which school and sport, in concert, shackle youth and limit opportunity. This is particularly problematic given that sport is so often celebrated as a means, perhaps the best chance, for many youth to attend college. The promise of an education for these kids is often just that, a promise that goes unfulfilled. Once that the promise of an education is experienced by athletes as insincere and/or at least difficult to realize, these individuals grow cynical and critical of their place in the space of sport in school.

Ernest's turn towards scholarship and away from college sport also began during his junior year, when his selection of English as a major represented for him "his first truly academic decision in his life." Like Malo, Ernest began to see himself as a scholar becoming. Others appreciated his academic potential as well. He met for coffee with professors who seemed genuinely interested in what he thought and had to say. He was more than a poster boy for the athletic department, and in fact, Ernest did have something to say. For it was the development of a racial and political consciousness that led Ernest to fully embrace a scholarly identity. It would also become the foundation for his research on critical pedagogy and social justice and making a difference in the lives of urban youth. Like Derek, whose research married the experiences of an emerging gay identity with that of a young scholar, Ernest's burgeoning scholarship focused on his own development as a politicized black man seeking equity and access for all youth. Ernest's fluidity and grace of movement within the academy demonstrated an intentional positioning of himself as a respected scholar and educator rather than being positioned as a black athlete getting an education.

Retelling Sport Narratives

Part of Ernest's becoming a political and critical scholar of education came from his frustrations with the way in which his own experiences in the academy had positioned him and labeled him as the idealized black student-athlete on a predominantly white campus. He shared this experience with Malo as an African American male athlete in college, but their experiences as black males was similar to Tony's as a white working-class college football player. While Ernest and Malo felt that they were intentionally limited within schools to pursue academics, Tony felt that such pursuits were a luxury he could ill afford. For Tony, it came down to what he called viable alternatives. He said, "for me I didn't have any viable alternatives…This goes into stuff that we were talking about, about opportunities and options, that it can't just be a way out. Sports just as a way out, then most of the people that I knew generally got out and ended up going back. When I was first here, some of my best friends were from Louisiana, black guys from the country, who you could barely understand, but we had this similar rural world-view that put us in concert. We were in some kind of classes, some beginning class they put us in. And we would all get into the game, and they have gone back, a couple of them didn't make it, my two roommates flunked out, it was just, there really wasn't a lot to keep you out, once you got out, staying out.…That's what I mean, if sports is just a way out, where do you go when you get out? Other than…there has got to be more. People are hurting, they have the sport experience, but there is got to be a way to make it more full."

Ernest picked up on this idea of sport as a vehicle of social mobility and personal freedom. But he spoke from his unique perspective as an African American male: "that's the danger of the whole metaphor of sport as a way out. That one day you're talking about getting out and stepping out of bounds, but once you get out, you realize that there is no place to go to. Either forward or backwards…I went out and there was nothing out there, but then when I tried to turn around and go back, I realized there was nothing there either. So

I was nowhere. You talk about space, and there is no person in outer space like a former athlete with no other options." In contrast to Tony, Ernest and Malo, Derek grew up in a white, middle class neighborhood, where, according to Derek, "sport was recreation from the real world. Few in the neighborhood viewed sport as a viable vocation." These men's vastly different sporting experiences illustrate where one world meets another, construed as very real by those living within these social spaces.

As Jabari summarized during one of the most dynamic dialogic meetings of the *Out of Bounds* meetings, "all of you guys have pointed out the space thing, and I'd like to come back to that. That's why I liked the 'out-of-bounds' metaphor, and originally, I think we talked about the court as a space, and the field as a space, and the de-realized space that has certain qualities to it. But this idea of boundaries, everyone has sort of talked about being bound by the protocols and the paradigms inside the sport, and in some cases that came as a slave-like binding, you were shackled into the sport. And even in Tony's experience it was similar in that there was nothing else. So even if you escape those boundaries and became unbound, had to do with manhood and other things, and we talked about games, and Derek's ability to have other things outside those bounds that made his shackles less binding. And there is a window that we're talking about here that I don't think has to be the ability of a person to have resources financially, although that certainly has its place, but everyone is not gonna be wealthy....But the question is what other cultural capital, and social capital, and intellectual capital is available to students, and to what extent was Emily Dickinson another capital place where you could go, a space to go, you could go into that attic with her, and have a place where those shackles are removed....It was an intellectual way of stepping-out-of-bounds into another bounded space, but I like this idea of "borrowed wings" because to get out of this boundary and into the attic, you had to have some way of elevating yourself and that those wings were said to be borrowed...is a comment on you and your sense of not being able to take ownership of the ability to take flight. So what we're looking for is how to instill in kids the fact that you can be rooted and have wings at the same time."

Tony's own sense of marginalization led him to want to take flight, to free himself from feeling shackled. As a working-class white male athlete, he could relate more fully with facets of the lived experiences of Ernest and Malo than he could with Derek. He found a kinship in their shared sense of subjugation and the pain of being positioned in the space of sport and school. In their own unique ways, these three men felt alienated and exploited by the schools and universities they attended. Ernest and Malo, independently in their initial writings, reflected on their sport experiences in school as a form of slavery or indentured servitude. Sport was hard work, not fun and games. They felt that they were valued for being athletes, first and foremost. Tony was initially uncomfortable with the metaphor of slavery used to describe Ernest and Malo's experiences in school and sport. But he could relate to their perceived sense of purpose within these educational institutions. As a revenue-athlete himself, Tony understood well the commodification of his athletic body. He too felt exploited and used. But the word slave was particularly powerful in describing the commodification of black bodies, so articulately described by Ernest and Malo.

There was a certain bondage of expectation, steering them towards sport and away from an academic identification. And the expectation began early in the lives of these two black men. Ernest recalled having his masculinity challenged by coaches and teammates, despite being "just a kid at the time." The process of using sport as a primary masculinity-validating experience can be particularly pronounced for young black men, who have traditionally been excluded from other mainstream expressions of masculinity such as economic success, positions of authority, etc. (Edwards, 1985).

Being positioned away from intellectual practices and towards sport contributed to a less than critical perspective. After all, it was the boy's body that mattered, the dichotomous structuring of black bodies and sharp minds. If the boy was too confident, meaning articulate, thoughtful, critical, it meant he was uncoachable. Better to keep the young men insecure by controlling and positioning them as exchangeable athletes in the field of sport. And what better way to bind kids than to make them believe that sport was their best and perhaps only way out, the best way to free one's existing shackles. Tony's reflection of Malo's sense of enslavement in sport captured this hegemonic process poignantly. Tony wrote, "What strikes me more…is the context where he felt enslaved—sport that is offered up as the pinnacle of freedom and success." Sport seldom offered a way out. Nor did sport nurture a freedom of expression, a critical perspective. Popular slogans of sport, such as "Be obedient; don't ask questions." "Do as you're told; be a team player." This kind of discourse supported a hierarchical structuring within sport organizations and conditioned individuals against critical thought (Sage, 1998).

Complicit in this dumbing down of intellectual potential were schools themselves. The educational system often supported positioning these students as non-students, particularly those African American youth who showed an inclination towards athletics. Malo was the first in his family to attend college. Despite his tremendous academic successes in high school, he was often expected to be an athlete first and a student second. The color of his skin, his black body, served as a beacon for the football coach at his high school to seek him and other African American youth out. It was difficult for youth to resist this symbolic investment in the social value attributed to their athletic potential. This imposed positioning led Malo to internalize his perceived worth. He wrote, "Without athletics, I was just exposed. What was I *really* about"? Teachers and coaches alike continued to reinforce this unidimensional athletic identity.

And as Ernest pointed out, many black youth accepted being defined primarily, if not solely, as athletes. This academic dis-identification seemed to only strengthen during adolescence, when constructions of self were most vulnerable to social expectation and peer pressure. As he reflected on this period in his life, Ernest earned the respect of his other black teammates in high school "by dunking a basketball, not by getting a 4.0 GPA." Being good at basketball, dominating the rim and others on the court, meant that you were *the man*. Even if you were not the dominant male of the group, sport provided a vehicle to express and enjoy the social benefits of masculinity. School didn't offer such symbolic value. Thus, many of the African American athletes that Ernest knew growing up had no intention of becoming good students, let alone scholars.

A glaring implication of this work, then, is to change not only the language of sport but also its larger narrative within American society. As parents, pastors, administrators, teachers, coaches, as peers and friends, we need to have a new story about the outcomes of sports participation. The idea that sport will make you rich and famous, that it is a way out of poverty and social invisibility, is an idea that deserves more than statistical scrutiny. The odds of making it to the professional ranks are strikingly low, but telling kids these odds does not seem to change their motivation to choose sport over other more realistic avenues for growth and development. The scrutiny needs to be more social, challenging the ways that we unconsciously promote this American rags-to-riches story—Horatio Alger in high tops.

If the way out involves education for these young athletes, it does little good to pass undeserving students through school, simply because teachers and administrators do not want to stand in their way of using sport to get ahead. These educators contribute to making both education and this particular vehicle for social mobility a mockery. It perpetuates the mind/body divide, contributing to the idea that these young people need not focus on academic and intellectual practices and undermines the quality and integrity of American education.

There are several other possible and positive outcomes of athletic participation other than getting out and moving up. Sport provides an opportunity for individuals to look internally, to find a balance between activities of the mind and body and experience a spirited, even spiritual, sense of oneself. This may also mean limiting the focus on an outward persona or appearance, building up a shell and a performative body, conditioned for use and commodification. Image is not everything, as the Canon advertisement featuring Andre Agassi told us in 1990. Depth of character and a holistic balance are important too. As social agents rather than sports agents, we need to help young people stop being texted and scripted to pursue a particular narrative without turning a critical lens back upon our own practices in the field of sport. Current and former athletes who have experienced this balance would give back more to their communities if they could use their symbolic capital and successful sport image as a way in with kids, to teach, educate, and make positive change.

Safe Spaces to Play and Learn

For Anne and Erin, their presence on the basketball court and soccer field challenged the social construction of masculinity. The challenge was more pronounced than merely entering a space historically dominated by men. These young women were literally competing against men, not only for the right to play; they were competing to win and to take men on physically. A woman physically dominating a male in the field of play had rich symbolic consequences. When a woman rises above a man, even temporarily, in a historically and socially scripted male domain such as sport, constructions of gender are heavily scrutinized, making both men and women ill at ease. It is not only men who have worked to keep women marginalized in the space of sports. Women, themselves, often were the strongest inhibitors of other women's expressions of liberation and agency. Responses to such challenges of social expectation can be violent, eliciting real acts of intimidation and aggression as well as symbolic acts of violence.

As demonstrated in the experiences of Anne and Erin in sport with and against men, their articulation of themselves as competent and competing athletes brought out displays of bravado and hyper-masculinity in their male teammates and opponents. Erin's successful shot block of one male opponent on a public basketball court revealed masculine insecurities manifested in a variety of troubling ways. When the man's claims of being fouled fell on deaf ears among those on the court, he reverted to rough play and physical intimidation. That she was a "girl" and not a man evoked a sense of public humiliation in this male rather than simply acknowledging a strong and skillful defensive play. The actual threat of violence led Erin to not feel safe, prompting her to stop play-ing with men altogether. By creating an unwelcome and unsafe space, this one male player was able to force a competent female athlete out of any future competitions.

While Erin faced physical intimidation by a man on a basketball court, Anne endured the verbal aggression of male soccer players against whom she competed. The term "Git the Skirt" came to represent the misogynist language of sport and the symbolic violence of men on women. The need to "git" her ele-vated the act of simply defending a player to a far more aggressive level. Male tales of their sexual exploits and locker room banter among her own teammates reinforced how the language and space of sport was neither open nor comfort-able for women.

Thus, while sport was conceived as a way out for Ernest, Malo and Tony, other men (and women) attempted to push or force out Erin and Anne by engaging in acts of real and symbolic violence. These acts of violence have his-torically led many women to elect out of sport, or at least sports that have come to be associated with so-called masculine characteristics. For as Lenskyj asserts (1993: 280), "athleticism is so clearly defined as a male attribute that its pres-ence in women is automatically assumed to 'masculinize' her, if she was not 'masculine' at the outset." In order to balance an emerging gender identity with an athletic identity, then, many women have chosen not to compete in sports at all in order to project a less conflicted image of femininity. If they do par-ticipate, many female teams respond by constructing a culture of hyper-femininity and homophobia. This was the case for Anne, playing on a Division I women's soccer team. For a lesbian athlete on such a team, this space becomes likewise unsafe and alienating. Thus, Anne could not be forced out by the sym-bolic violence and expressions of hyper-masculinity she experienced playing with the boy's soccer team in high school. However, the compulsory heterosex-uality and hyper-femininity of her women's college soccer team ultimately led her to give up her athletic scholarship and quit the team.

Like Anne, Derek was confronted with the hegemonic masculinity of sport, which marginalizes and subordinates both women and gay men. He cap-tained his professional soccer team as a closeted gay man. But as Anne's story reveals, the hyper-femininity which arose as a corollary to this hegemonic masculinity similarly marginalized her as a lesbian athlete on a women's team. Thus, the space and language of sport can be an uncomfortable and unsafe place for individuals who do not play by the social rules of an imposed gender order. Thus, within the binary construction of the gender order, boys participating in purportedly "girls' games" and girls participating in so-called "boys' games" become socially stigmatized. So too are gay boys and lesbian girls participating in sports which impose an imperative around compulsory heterosexuality. They are either silenced and limited in their range of motion, or they must leave the space to move in directions which allow for a greater freedom of expression.

While these stories illustrate how sport can be an unsafe space for many, so too can the classroom be alienating, rife with symbolic acts of violence against students. Despite their proven track records in school, the African American members of the *Out of Bounds* group were negatively tracked in class-rooms by teachers who had lowered expectations of their academic ability. These lowered expectations were far more pronounced for the three black members of the group than they were for the three white participants. Ernest, Malo and Erin each wrote and spoke about these painful experiences as they fought to be recognized as serious students who desired to become scholars. Earning top marks and being offered academic scholarships to èlite universities did not seem to discourage these lowered expectations.

Erin's mother had to fight to make sure that she was not placed in lower-tracked classes at her private elementary school attended primarily by wealthy white children. Malo described feeling invisible as a student with a gnawing "fear of just being a nobody." As the only African American students in many of their honors classes throughout school, they felt isolated. Ernest reported that he "did not feel safe in any other persona than a hard-core athlete." Frequently asked what sport they played by strangers on the predominantly white univer-sity campuses they attended, Ernest and Malo learned quickly that the space of school projected superior athletic expectations onto them in addition to the lowered expectations in the classroom.

Erin and her family held high expectations for her academic achievement. She didn't disappoint. By the third grade, she already wanted to get a Ph.D. She scored in the top one percent of her age group at this time, but the school still tried to keep her out of honors classes. In her honors English class in middle school, Erin was accused of cheating because she had earned the highest grade in the class.

As noted in chapter three, the response of several white graduate students in one of Jabari's seminars on literacy at Berkeley was particularly telling when they were confronted with the expectation of understanding a discourse alien to their background and current knowledge. When Ernest's and Jeff's high school students from Oakland quizzed the graduate students about hip-hop music and culture on an in-class test, several graduate students voiced concern that they should not be subjected to such tests and that the experience was uncomfortable. Of course, these students were uncomfortable largely because they were unfamiliar with the language of hip-hop and could not excel on a test given to them by these high school students. They were perhaps also uncomfortable with the inversion of normal power relations within the classroom, these younger students of color owning and controlling the code or school-sanctioned discourse, albeit temporarily. One white female graduate student's response to Jabari that she did not feel safe in the classroom highlights the ways in which certain styles of teaching and learning are deemed safe in the classroom while others are not. This forces us to confront why the structures and cultures of school differentially impact students, their level of comfort and safety, and their sense of belonging or not.

These examples of individuals feeling unsafe in both sport and school suggest that as educators we must strive to create welcoming and open spaces to learn and to foster a freedom to play without restriction. This responsibility rests with individual teachers and coaches who must be conscious and self-reflective about the social and physical environments they create for the exercises of the mind and body. But so too does the responsibility of safety rest with administrators of schools and organizations in analyzing the social and physical geography of institutions in and through which our youth pass.

A clear implication of these lived experiences is the need to teach children, regardless of race, social class, gender or sexuality, the respective rules of the game. If students in classrooms or youth in sport are not provided the parameters and tools for success, they are doomed to fail and feel out of place. This suggests that as adults and educators we must not take our understanding of these rules for granted, helping youth experience and become competent and confident in their engagement with academic and athletic discourses. But so too must we vigilantly seek to make the rules fair for all participants rather than favoring the few over the many. Perhaps one way to promote fair play and safe spaces for all is to begin focusing our collective attention on, and celebration of, assists rather than scores. While scores symbolize competition and the victory of the few, assists represent collaboration and working towards a common goal. The shift of focus does not imply that there will be no competition or individuality, but that achievement might be a more shared experience.

On his website regarding the positive coach mental model, Jim Thompson challenges the win-at-all-costs mentality in youth sports and society at large by seeking to redefine what it means to be a winner. He wrote, "a positive coach helps players redefine what it means to be a winner through a mastery, rather than a scoreboard, orientation. He sees victory as a by-product of the pursuit of excellence. He focuses on effort rather than outcome and on learning rather than comparison to others. He recognizes that mistakes are an important and inevitable part of learning and fosters an environment in which players don't fear making mistakes. While not ignoring the teaching opportunities that mistakes present, he teaches players that a key to success is how one responds to mistakes. He sets standards of continuous improvement for himself and his players. He encourages his players, whatever their level of ability, to strive to become the best players, and people, they can be. He teaches players that a winner is someone who makes maximum effort, continues to learn and improve, and doesn't let mistakes (or fear of mistakes) stop them." (from The Positive Coach Mental Model website)

This redefined understanding of a winner may equally apply to students, who are often trained and disciplined to win at all costs in the classroom. Grades become the coveted currency of exchange and academic performance is measured by a comparison with others rather than an intrinsic desire to learn. The implication for education is clear: like coaches adopting a positive coaching model for youth sports, teachers might utilize a positive pedagogy focused on learning and mastery, where intelligence is understood to be developed rather than fixed. And as discussed previously in this chapter, different styles of learning and types of intelligence might likewise be rewarded such as a kinesthetic understanding of the world and our place within that world.

Redefining Sport in Schools

The functional reading of a game or sport, governed by physical boundaries and codified rules, can also be understood as a space embodying play of deeper meaning and cultural significance. As noted in the introduction, Bourdieu's (1991) conception of a field or game recognizes this space as a site of struggles among individuals seeking to maintain or alter the distribution of society's resources or spoils. He differentiated between these resources, recognizing that in addition to material wealth in the form of money and property or what has been referred to as economic capital, there likewise exists a struggle for cultural and symbolic capital. It is these struggles that deepen our understanding or reading of the game. Cultural capital refers to knowledge and technical skills, acquired most commonly through education and training. Symbolic capital refers more broadly to accumulated prestige or honor. As Thompson (1991) argued, "one of the most important properties of fields is the way in which they allow one form of capital to be converted into another—in the way, for example, that certain educational qualifications can be cashed in for lucrative jobs" (14). Although it is most commonly understood that these educational qualifications refer primarily to academic credentials, the training and discipline of the athletic body may likewise be exchanged as a marketable commodity. This is how the space of sport becomes viewed as a vehicle for social and economic mobility. The privileged position of athletes in society and within educational institutions is evidence of a symbolic capital as demonstrated by status, popularity, and prestige.

Student-athletes' institutional relationships with schools and universities support the very legitimacy of these educational institutions, at least externally. By representing their schools, they become the symbolic bearers of an institutional identity. They represent the school in competition with other like institutions, wearing the colors, the crest, and supporting the conservative trappings of their schools. The support bestowed upon them by fans within and outside of the school borders is also support bestowed upon the institution. And yet, their athletic participation as school-sanctioned activity is argued to undermine its educational mission at many institutions. Thus, the symbolic capital enjoyed by student-athletes and their respective institutions due to athletic achievement often comes with a corresponding contempt and disdain.

The space of sports is but one field or game, but its relationship to schools is no coincidence, according to Bourdieu (1978). The very rise of modern sport, states the author, "took place in the educational establishments reserved for the 'èlites' of bourgeois society, the English public schools, where the sons of aristocratic or upper-bourgeois families took over a number of *popular*—i.e. *vulgar*—*games*, simultaneously changing the meaning and function in exactly the same way as the field of learned music transformed the folk dances— bourrées, sarabands, gavottes, etc.—which it introduced into the high-art forms such as the suite" (823).

The emergence of intercollegiate athletics within American educational institutions in the mid-nineteenth century was similarly founded on the classist premise of amateurism, playing simply for the love of the game with no material aim. Bourdieu (1978) noted, "what is acquired in and through experience of school, a sort of retreat from the world and from real practice, of which the great boarding schools of the 'èlite' represent the fully developed form, is the propensity towards activity for no purpose, a fundamental aspect of the ethos of bourgeois 'èlites' who always pride themselves on disinterestedness and define themselves by an elective distance—manifested in art and sport—from material interests" (823–824). This bourgeois approach to sport and school is powerfully reflected in Derek's narrative as a middle class soccer player, who wrote of sport as a diversion from real life. His lived experience with soccer was no rags-to-riches narrative; he had not suffered economic hardship in his youth and American soccer hardly offered riches, as it represents a sport played primarily by middle class youth and adults competing in recreational leagues. He embodied the philosophy of amateurism even when he played professionally. Derek was more serious about school. Education was highly valued in his family. Education, not sport, was a more rational investment in future opportunity. It led him to make decisions along his journey to prioritize school over sport. He studied abroad while in college, missing his junior year season, despite being the captain of the team the year prior. He was leading by example on and off the field and his example boldly stated that school is as important, if not more so, than sports.

This class reading of Derek as a white upper-middle class soccer player might also be applicable to Anne and Erin, based upon their academic identities. Neither woman had expectations to play their sport professionally. While there exist women's professional leagues for both basketball (WNBA) and soccer (WPS), neither Anne nor Erin seemed particularly motivated to use sport as a vehicle for social and economic mobility. There certainly are young women today who pursue sport as a means to such ends, but the American narrative of sport is popularized primarily as a story for boys and men. The narratives of Anne, Erin and Derek reveal that middle class, Olympic or non-revenue student-athletes are in many ways similar to female student-athletes in their respective relationship to sport and school. But while Anne and Erin were both gifted academically and athletically, their engagements as women in sport and school were significantly different, based upon their own understandings and experiences of race, class and sexuality.

As we have discussed earlier in this chapter, Ernest, Malo and Erin all grew up in families that highly valued the pursuit of education. Due to a mosaic of factors, many of the educational institutions they attended had lower expectations of their academic worth and potential relative to other students in their classes. That each of these individuals was African American, and that each of these individuals was gifted athletically, contributed at least as much, if not more, to these lowered expectations in school as did their social class. And yet, as black males, Ernest and Malo had qualitatively different experiences with sport in school than did Erin, a black female. Their sense of being enslaved, even for Malo on an academic and not an athletic scholarship, highlights the depth of emotion undergirding these individuals' narratives.

Tony, on the other hand, knew he would play professional football by the eighth grade. Raised in poverty, left alone to fend for himself as a fifth grader, Tony would use his physical size and athletic skills to enhance his future opportunities. The sport of football became his ticket out. Football would take him to a university as a heavily recruited athlete. Football would take him to the league, the National Football League, where he would embody the American narrative of sport and social mobility, a rags-to-riches story enacted by a poor, white kid. It would be overly simplistic, however, to suggest that Tony was not well aware of his intellectual abilities and potential. He knew he was smart. What he did not know at that time was that he could have done almost anything with such potential. Because of the strength and size of his body, he was being moved towards sport at an early age. It was made clear to him that his body was valuable. And so, he used his body for what it was worth. When his body finally broke down due to injuries and it would take him no further athletically, he returned to school and the exercises of the mind, something he had previously deemed a luxury. He had always had the potential for intellectual exercise, but he had not really been given the chance. Once in graduate school, Tony still questioned his return to the university and an intentional but conflicted turn towards scholarship. As he wrote at that time, "there are issues of entitlement and privilege associated with being a scholar." He was working through where he had been, where he was going, and what alternative space he might inhabit.

As demonstrated in the dialogic data of the *Out of Bounds* process, the differences between these four men and two women were as telling as their surface similarities. For these former athletes as scholars becoming, race and gender combined with social class and sexuality to create qualitatively different lived experiences. As their stories revealed, the participants' membership within seemingly static and fixed social categories imposed relative expectations and opportunities in both school and sport. But these narratives likewise showed that there is differential power and privilege within these social categories, suggesting a more fluid reading of our lived experiences and the multiple positions we simultaneously inhabit.

Opening the Field of Play

In the early 1970s, the Dutch premier soccer team, Ajax of Amsterdam, developed a strategy of play known as total football (Totaalvoetbal). The concept of total football or soccer became world renowned largely because of the team's unprecedented success. Ajax won the coveted European Cup from 1971–1973, as well as taking the European Treble in 1972, three top tournaments in a single year. But total football also gained attention around the world because of its novelty; it was a different way of conceiving the field and the movement of players on the field. The strategic premise of total football involves the opening of space to offer the greatest fluidity of positions relative to one another.

Within this open system, no player's position is fixed; each player is presumed to be able to take on a number of different positions as the game develops organically and fluidly. The success of the system had to do with the creation of open space, allowing for such mobility. As Ajax defender Barry Hulschoff, who played on the team that won three consecutive European Cups, noted, "It was about making space, coming into space, and organizing space" (http://news.bbc.co.uk/sportacademy/hi/sa/football/features/newsid_3301000/3301407.stm). It is of little surprise that total football became associated with opening the field of play and making the beautiful game truly beautiful.

A recurring theme throughout the narratives of these four men and two women was the way in which each of the *Out of Bounds* participants felt positioned within the space of sport and school. Being positioned presumes a structural determination of mobility, limiting the possibilities of becoming and actualizing alternative trajectories. Whether racialized, gendered, commodified or objectified, whether physicalized or invisibilized, the fields of sport and school often hindered the mobility of these young men and women. Many of the informants described feeling out of place, alienated, and unwelcome in these spaces. At times, due to real and symbolic acts of violence against them, these participants felt unsafe.

In addition to educators and institutions taking greater responsibility for creating safe spaces for all youth, so too should we encourage and promote a playful and open spirit in the classroom and in sport. Too often, the informants described their academic and athletic experiences as forced and unfulfilling labor, working to fit in, feeling alienated and isolated. The emotional and physical pain associated with feeling bound and shackled seemed the antithesis of the freedom inherent in play. It certainly did not sound like the freedom and beauty described in total football where spaces were opened for multiple players to take on multiple positions.

We are rooted in our life histories and a desire for coherence. We want to tell ourselves and others that we are whole, agentic, intentional. As Mills (1959) contended, "no social study that does not come back to the problems of biography, of history and of their intersections within a society has completed its intellectual journey" (12). Our own narratives are lived within larger social narratives and structures of power and privilege, where social categories of race, class, gender, and sexuality collude and collide.

As described in the introduction, the image of the tree or root has pervasively implanted a binary logic within western thought. This cultural notion has led to the reproduction of artificial and oppositional dualisms. In an attempt to see better the forest through the trees, we have used the concept of the rhi-zome (Deleuze and Guattari, 1987), which suggests a multiplicity of connec-tions and a heterogeneity of thinking and being. The collected data of individual life histories, combined with the shared interpretation of personal narratives and artifacts, provided a more open and democratic process of com-munication. The dialogic process also revealed a multiplicity of ways of becom-ing, turning from being athletes primarily to being scholars and educators. The dialogic process, then, complicated the lived experiences of these four men and two women, suggesting that there was no singular way to make this acad-emic move; rather, there were many paths to similar destinations of scholarship. In the process, these two women and four men freed their minds to pursue intel-lectual and creative work, becoming to realize a sound mind in a sound body.

Both sport and school create a structured space within which identities interact both on the social as well as somatic levels. The social construction of identity through participation in these fields will inevitably be shaped by the particular cultural and historical conditions. These conditions are affected at all times by the reigning structure of power within and between cultural iden-tities based upon race, class, gender, and sexuality. As such, the determination of who possesses the social power to participate within these social practices (i.e., the power to play, which positions to inhabit, as well as the strategies and tactics of play) depends upon the historical structures confining or affirming social and physical mobility within particular spaces. However, players as active agents continually confront these cultural systems of power, at times tres-passing within spaces previously thought closed to them, culturally forbidden arenas of activity.

The rules and parameters of play often seem fixed, but as the stories of our informants have illustrated, the intentional stepping out of bounds often clar-ifies just exactly where the boundaries exist. This intentional move towards self-clarification helps inform others as well. Anne's decision to leave her college soccer team because she found that it was not an open field of play helped other members of the team know where they stood as well and set them in motion in new directions. That several other members of the team, both gay and straight, also quit the team suggests that her actions revealed how the bound-aries of play were limiting and exclusive.

By understanding the boundaries and the rules of play, we are able to see the field for what it is and what it might become in the future. Stepping out of bounds, then, is the conscious and critical act of playing with these boundaries and rules in order to become who and what we want to become. In the space of sport and schools, there needs to be more room to play. It need not be situated solely in a gymnasium or an èlite space reserved for the few. While play remains grounded within a restricted and objective range of possibilities, a "moving unity of subjectivity and objectivity" (Sartre, 1968: 97; Ortner, 1996: 20), play promises the possibility of human liberation, however transitory, in the face of structural constraints. As educators, we can celebrate play in the classroom and in sport—play with ideas and activity in learning. This shift re-conceives learning as an end in itself and not as a means to an undisclosed end. We can make learning and playing a luxury available to all, not just a privileged few. In this effort, we will open the game to allow for greater participation of players of all abilities and social positions. The process of opening celebrates the fluidity of different positions in the fields of sport and school. Such fluidi-ty allows for individuals to have greater mobility in their lives; in turn, we will expand our cultural understanding of being and of becoming whole.

· 1 ·

REFERENCES

Adler, P. A., & Adler, P. (1987) Role conflict and identity salience: College athletics and the academic role. *The Social Science Journal*, 24, 443–455.

———. (1991). *Backboards and blackboards: College athletes and role engulfment*. New York: Columbia University Press.

Andrews, V. L. (1996). Black bodies-white control: The contested terrain of sportsmanlike conduct. *Journal of African American Men*, Summer 1996, 2:1, pps. 33–59.

Aronowitz, S. and Giroux, H. A. (1991). *Postmodern education: Politics, culture, and social criticism*. Minneapolis: University of Minnesota Press.

Associated Press. (2001, February 21). Disbelief in teens' town: Dartmouth slaying suspects seen as regular guys. *San Francisco Chronicle*, p. A3.

Bacon, R. K. (1997, July). Court of last resort: Sports, race, and the common ground. *Express Books*, pp. 1–9.

Bakhtin, M. M. (1981). *The dialogic imagination*. Translated by Michael Holquist. Austin: University of Texas Press.

Beyond Sports. http://www.youtube.com/watch?v=ieOnJfWYZRY. Retrieved 2009-09-08.

Bogdan, R. and Biklen, S. (1992). *Qualitative research for education: An introduction to theory and methods*. Boston: Allyn and Bacon.

Bourdieu, P. (1977). *Outline of a theory of practice*. (R. Nice, Trans.). Cambridge, U.K.: Cambridge University Press.

———. (1978). Sport and social class. *Social Science Information*, 17(6), 819–840.

———. (1990). Programme for a sociology of sport. *In other words: Essays towards a reflexive sociology*. Stanford: Stanford University Press.

———. (1991). *Language and symbolic power*. Cambridge, Mass.: Harvard University Press.

Bowen, W. G. and Levin, S.A. (2003). *Reclaiming the game: College sports and educational values*. Princeton, NJ: Princeton University Press.

Brodley, L. (1987). Writing critical ethnographic narratives. *Anthropology and Education Quarterly* 18, 67–76.

Byers, W. and Hammer, C.H. (1995). *Unsportsmanlike conduct: Exploiting college athletes*. Ann Arbor: University of Michigan Press.

Byrne, B.M., & Shavelson, R.J. (1986). On the structure of adolescent self concept. *Journal of Educational Psychology*, 78, 474–481.

Carrigan, T., Connell, B. and Lee, J. (1987). Toward a new sociology of masculinity. In H. Brod (Ed.) *The making of masculinities: The new men's studies*. Boston: Allen and Unwin.

Carter, P. (1992). *Living in a new country: History, traveling and language*. London: Faber & Faber.

Choudhury, S., Blakewood, S., & Charman, T. (2006). *Social cognitive development during adolescence*. London: Oxford University Press

Casey, K. (1995). The new narrative research in education. In M. W. Apple (Ed.) *Review of Research in Education*, 21, pp. 211–253.

Chu, D. (1989). *The Character of American Higher Education & Intercollegiate Sport*. Albany: State University of New York Press.

Coakley, J. J. (2004). Sport in society: Issues & controversies. 8th ed. Boston: McGraw-Hill.

Connell, R.W. 1987. *Gender and power*. Stanford, CA: Stanford University Press.

Covington, M. (1992). *Making the grade: Self-worth perspective on motivation and school reform*. Cambridge: Cambridge University Press.

Cronan, M.K., & Scott, D. (2008). Triathlon and women's narratives of bodies and sport. *Leisure Sciences*, 30, 17–34.

Csordas, T. J. (1989). Embodiment as a paradigm for anthropology. *Ethos*, 18, 5–47.

Damon, W., & Hart, D. (1988). *Self-understanding in childhood and adolescence*. New York: Cambridge University Press.

Deleuze, G. and Guattari, F. (1987). *A thousand plateaus: Capitalism and schizophrenia*. Minneapolis, MN: The University of Minnesota Press.

DeMott, B. (2005). Jocks and the academy. *New York Review of Books*, 52: 8.

Dewey, J. (1961, c.1900). *The school and society*. Chicago: University of Chicago Press.

Diemer, M. & Blustein, D. (2005). Critical consciousness and career development among urban youth. (Available online August 2006).

Douglas, M. (1978). *Natural symbols: Explorations in cosmology*. New York: Praeger.

Drewery, W., & Monk, G. (1994). Some reflections on the therapeutic power of poststructuralism. *International Journal for the Advancement of Counseling*, 17, 303–313.

Duderstadt, J.J. (2000). *Intercollegiate athletics and the American university: A university president's perspective*. Ann Arbor; University of Michigan Press.

Dyson, M. E. (1993). *Reflecting black: African American cultural criticism*. Minneapolis: University of Minnesota Press.

Eckert, P.. (1989). *Jocks and burnouts: Social categories and identity in the high school*. New York: Teachers College Press.

Edwards, H. (1973). *Sociology of sport*. Homewood, Ill.: Dorsey.

———. (1985). Educating black athletes. In D. Chu, J. O. Segrave, & B. J. Becker (Eds.), *Sport and higher education* (pp. 373–384). Champaign: Human Kinetics.

Eitzen, D. S. (2000), September 26–30). Slaves of big time college sports. *USA Today*. 29,26–30.

Entine, J. (2000). *Taboo: Why black athletes dominate sports and why we're afraid to talk about it.* New York: Public Affairs.

Erikson, E.H. (1968). *Identity: Youth and crisis.* New York: W.W. Norton.

Fairclough, N. (1992). *Discourse and social change.* Oxford, UK: Blackwell.

Fanell, B. (1999). Moving bodies, acting selves. *Annual Review of Anthropology*, 28, 341–373.

Ferdman, B.M. (1990). Literacy and cultural identity. *Harvard Educational Review*, 60, 181–204.

Fitzgerald, A. (1997, December 29). It's the mind that matters in the NBA. *San Francisco Chronicle*, p. C8.

Foucault, M. (1977). *Discipline and punish.* (A. Sheridan, Trans.). Harmondsworth: Penguin.

Freeberg, L. (1993, January 26). Stanford president challenges sanctity of degree. *San Francisco Chronicle*, p. A1.

Garcia, L., Hart, D., & Johnson-Ray, R. (1997). What do children and adolescents think about themselves? A developmental account of self-concept. In S. Hala (Ed.), *The development of social cognition*. East Sussex, UK: Psychology Press.

Gee, J. P. (1990) *Social linguistics and literacies: Ideology in discourses.* Bristol, PA: Falmer.

Gilroy, P. (1993). *The black Atlantic: Modernity and double consciousness.* Cambridge, MA: Harvard University Press.

Giroux, H. A. (1994). Living dangerously: Identity politics and the new cultural racism. In H. A. Giroux & P. McLaren (Eds.) *Between borders: Pedagogy and the politics of cultural studies.* New York: Routledge.

Goodson, I., & Dowbiggin, I. (1990). Docile bodies: Commonalities in the history of psychiatry and schooling. In S. Ball (Ed.), *Foucault and education: Disciplines and knowledge* (pp. 105–129). London: Routledge.

Gregory, A. and Weinstein, R. (2008). The discipline gap and African Americans: Defiance or cooperation in the high school classroom. *Journal of School Psychology*, 46, 455–475.

Haraway, D.J. (1991). *Simians, cyborgs, and women: The reinvention of nature.* New York: Routledge.

Harter, S. (1999). *The construction of self: A developmental perspective.* New York: Guilford Press

Hawkins, B. (2000). *The new plantation: The internal colonization of black student-athletes.* Winterville, GA: Sadiki Press.

Hoberman, J. (1997). *Darwin's athletes: How sport has damaged black America and preserved the myth of race.* Boston: Houghton Mifflin.

hooks, b. (1999). *Remembered rapture: The writer at work.* New York: Henry Holt.

Huizinga, J. (1950). *Homo Ludens: As study of the play element in culture.* Boston, MA: Beacon Press, 1950.

Hunter, I. (1992). Aesthetics and cultural studies. *Cultural Studies.* C. Grossberg, C. Nelson, and P.A. Treichler (Eds.), 347–372. New York: Routledge, 1992.

Kamler, B., Maclean, R., Reid, J., & Simpson, A. (1993). Shaping up nicely: The formation of schoolgirls and schoolboys in the first month of school, a report to the Gender Equity and Curriculum Reform Project, Department of Employment, Education and Training. Geelong: Deakin University Press.

Jones, A. (2000). Surveillance and student handwriting: Tracing the body. In C. O'Farrell, D. Meadmore, E. McWilliam, & C. Symes (Eds.), *Taught bodies* (pp. 151–164). New York: Peter Lang.

Lapsley, D.K., Milstead, M., Quintana, S.M., Flannery, D., & Buss, R.R. (1986). Adolescent ego-centrism and formal operations: Tests of a theoretical assumption. *Developmental Psychology*, 12, 269–288.

Laslett, B. and Thorne, B. (1997). Introduction. In B. Laslett & B. Thorne (Eds.), *Feminist sociology: Life histories of a movement* (pp. 1–27). New Jersey: Rutgers University Press.

Lenskyj, H. (1993). Jocks and Jills: Women's experience in sport and physical activity. In G. Finn (Ed.), *Limited Edition: Voices of women, voices of feminism* (pp. 266–285). Halifax, NS: Fernwood.

Lerner, R. & Steinberg, L. (Eds.), (2004). *Handbook of adolescent psychology*. (2nd Edition). Hoboken, NJ: John Wiley and Sons

Lock, M. (1993). Cultivating the body: Anthropology and epistemologies of bodily practice and knowledge. *Annual Review of Anthropology*, 22, 133–135.

Lyotard, J.F. (1984). *The postmodern condition: A report on knowledge*. (G. Bennington & B. Massumi, Trans.). Minneapolis: University of Minnesota Press.

Mahiri, J. (1998). *Shooting for excellence: African American and youth culture in new century schools*. New York: Teachers College Press and NCTE Press.

———. Everyday indignities. *San Francisco Chronicle*, Sept. 9, 2001. C5, p. 1.

Mahiri, J. and Conner, E. (2003). Black youth violence has a bad rap. *Journal of Social Issues*, 59 (1), 121–140.

Majors, R. (1990). Cool pose: Black masculinity and sports. In *Sport, men, and the gender order*. M. Messner and D. Sabo (Eds.). Champaign, IL: Human Kinetics Publishers, Inc., 109–114.

Marshall, J. (1994, November 12). Studies say that colleges exploit athletes. *San Francisco Chronicle*, E1–E8.

Marshall, J.D. (1996). *Michel Foucault: Personal autonomy and education*. Dordrecht: Kluwer Academic.

Martinez, D. (2008). Soccer in the USA: "Holding out for a hero"? *Soccer & Society*, 9, 231–243.

Merleau-Ponty, M. (1962). *Phenomenology of Perception*. London: Routledge.

Messner, M. A. (1987). The meaning of success: The athletic experience and the development of male identity. In H. Brod (Ed.), *The making of masculinities: The new men's studies*. Boston: Allen and Unwin.

———. (1990). When bodies are weapons: Masculinity and violence in sport. *International Review for the Sociology of Sport*, 25, 203–220.

———. (1992). *Power at play: Sports and the problem of masculinity*. Boston: Beach Press.

Meyer, B. B. (1990). From idealism to actualization: The academic performance of female college athletes. *Sociology of Sport Journal* 7: 44–57.

Mills, C. W. (1959). *The sociological imagination*. London: Oxford University Press.

Monk, G., Winslade, J., Crocket, K., & Epston, D. (1997). *Narrative therapy in practice: The archaeology of hope*. San Francisco: Jossey-Bass.

Montemayor, R. & Eisen, M. (1977). The development of self conceptions from childhood to adolescence. *Developmental Psychology*, 13, 314–349.

Morrell, E. & Duncan Andrade, J. (2004). What they do learn in school: Using hip-hop as a bridge to canonical poetry. In J. Mahiri (Ed.). *What they don't learn in school: Literacy in the lives of urban youth*. New York: Peter Lang.

Ortner, S. B. (1996). *Making gender: The politics and erotics of gender*. Boston: Beacon Press.

Pratt, M. L. (1992). *Imperial eyes: Travel and writing and transculturation*. New York: Routledge.

Purdy, D., Eitzen, D., & Hufnagel, L. (1982). Are athletes also students? *Social Problems*, 29, 439–448.

Rehberg, R. A., and Schafer, W. E. (1968, May). Participation in interscholastic athletics and college expectations. *The American Journal of Sociology*, 73: 6, 732–740.

Reischer, E., & Koo, K.S. (2004). The body beautiful: Symbolism and agency in the social world. *Annual Review of Anthropology*, 33, 297–317.

Rhoden, William C. (2006). *$40 million dollar slaves: The rise, fall, and redemption of the black athlete*. New York: Crown Publishers.

Riessman, C. K. (1993). *Narrative analysis*. Newbury Park, CA: Sage.

Rigauer, B. (1981). *Sport and work*. New York: Columbia University Press.

Robinson, T.L. (1999). The intersections of dominant discourses across race, gender and other identities. *Journal of Counseling and Development*, 77, 73–79.

Roediger, D. R. (1991). *The wages of whiteness: Race and the making of the American working class*. London: Verso.

Rosenberg, M. (1979). *Conceiving the self*. New York: Basic Books.

Rosenwald, G. C. & Ochberg, R. L. (1992). Introduction: Life stories, cultural politics, and self-understanding. In G.C. Rosenwald and R.L. Ochberg (Eds.) *Storied lives: The cultural politics of self understanding*. (pp. 1–18). New Haven, CT: Yale University Press.

Sabo, D. (1985). Sport, patriarchy, and male identity: New questions about men and sport. *Arena Review*, 9.

Sack, A. L., & Thiel, R. (1979). College football and social mobility: A Case study of Notre Dame football players. *Sociology of Education*, 52, 60–66.

Sage, G. H. (1998). *Power and ideology in American sport: A critical perspective*. Champaign, IL: Human Kinetics.

Sartre, J.P. (1968). *Search for a method*; Translated from French and with an introduction by Hazel E. Barnes. New York: Vintage Books.

Savage, H. J., Bentley, H. W., McGovern, J. T., & Smiley, D. F. (1929). *American college athletics*. (Bulletin 23). New York: Carnegie Foundation for the Advancement of Teaching.

Schafer, W. & Armer, J. M. (1968, November, 21–26, 61–62). Athletes are not inferior students. *Transaction*.

Scheper-Hughes, N., & Lock, M. (1987). The mindful body: A prolegomenon to future work in medical anthropology. *Medical Anthropology*.1, 6–41.

Shapiro, B. (1984). Intercollegiate athletic participation and academic achievement: A case study of Michigan State University student–athletes, 1950–1980. *Sociology of Sport Journal*, 1, 46–51.

Shulman, J. L., and Bowen, W.G. (2001). *The game of life: College sports and educational values*. Princeton, N.J.: Princeton University Press.

Simons, R. (1991) Intercollegiate athletics: Do they belong on campus? In J. Andre & D. James (Eds.). *Rethinking college athletics*. Philadelphia: Temple University Press.

Simons, H. & Van Rheenen, D. (2000). Noncognitive predictors of student athletes' academic performance . *Journal of College Reading and Learning* 30, 167–181.

Simons, H. (2003). Race and penalized sports behavior. *International Review of the Sociology of Sport*. 28:1, 5–22.

Snyder, E. E. (1985). A theoretical analysis of academic and athletic roles. *Sociology of Sport*

Journal 2, 210–217.

Snyder, E. E., and Spreitzer, E. (1992, June). Social psychological concomitants of adolescents' role identities as scholars and athletes: A longitudinal analysis. *Youth and Society*, 23:4, 507–522.

Sperber, M. (1999, January 8). In praise of "student-athletes": The NCAA is haunted by its past. *Chronicle of Higher Education*, A76.

Sperber, M. (2000). *Beer and circus: How big-time college sports is crippling undergraduate education.* New York: Henry Holt and Company.

Sport Academy. British Broadcasting Corporation. Johan Cruyff: The total footballer. http://news.bbc.co.uk/sportacademy/hi/sa/football/features/newsid_3301000/3301407.stm. Retrieved 2009-09-08.

Steele, C. M. (1992, April). Race and the schooling of Black Americans. *The Atlantic Monthly*, 68–76.

Storey, J. (1993). *An introductory guide to cultural theory and popular culture.* Athens: The University of Georgia Press.

Summer, L. (2003). *Learning joy from dogs without collars.* New York: Simon & Schuster.

Thelin, J. R. (1994). *Games colleges play: Scandal and reform in intercollegiate athletics.* Baltimore: The Johns Hopkins University Press.

Thompson, J. The positive coach mental model. http://www.positivecoach.org/subcontent. aspx?SecID=111. Retrieved 2009-09-08.

Thorne, B. (1993). *Gender play: Girls and boys in school.* New Brunswick, NJ: Rutgers University Press.

Turner, T. (1994). Bodies and anti-bodies: Flesh and fetish in contemporary social theory. *Ethos*, 24, 27–47.

Underwood, J. (1979). *The death of an American game.* Boston: Little Brown.

Van Rheenen, D. (2000). Boys who play hopscotch: The historical divide of a gendered space. Play and Culture Studies: Theories in Contest and Out, 3, 111-130.

———. (Fall, 2008). University of California. Student-athlete academic performance summary. Berkeley: University of California.

———. (2009). The promise of soccer in America: The open play of ethnic subcultures. *Soccer and Society*, 10, 781–794.

Van Wolputte, S. (2004). Hang on to your self: Of bodies, embodiment, and selves. *Annual Review of Anthropology*, 33, 251–269.

Vygotsky, L. S. (1978). *Mind in society: The development of higher psychological processes.* Michael Cole et al. (Eds.). Cambridge : Harvard University Press.

Vygotsky, S. L.(1987). Thinking and speech. In R.W. Riber & A.S. Carton (eds.), *The collected works of S.L. Vygotsky,* New York: Plenum.

Wacquant, L. (1995). Pugs at work: Bodily capital and bodily labour among professional boxers. *Body Sociology*, 11, 65–93.

Watkins, M. (June, 2005). The erasure of habit: Tracing the pedagogic body. *Discourse: Studies in the Cultural Politics of Education*, 26, 167–181.

Wideman, J. E. (1992, September). Dead black men and other fallout from the American dream. *Esquire*, pp. 149–156.

Willis, P. (1981). Cultural production is different from cultural reproduction is different from social reproduction is different from reproduction. *Interchange*, 12, 48–67.

———. (1990). *Common culture*. Boulder, CO: Westview Press.

Wilson, J. (1994). *Playing by the rules: Sport, society, and the state*. Detroit, MI: Wayne State University Press.

Winslade, J., Monk, G., & Drewery, W. (1997). Sharpening the critical edge: A social constructionist approach in counselor education. In T. Sexton & B. Griffin (Eds.), *Constructivist thinking in counseling practice, research and training*. New York: Teachers College, Columbia University.

Zimbalist, Andew (2001). Unpaid professionals: The student as athlete. In Eitzen, D. Stanley. *Sport in contemporary society. An anthology*. Sixth Edition. New York: St. Martin's Press, 213–218.

Studies in the Postmodern Theory of Education

General Editors
Joe L. Kincheloe & Shirley R. Steinberg

Counterpoints publishes the most compelling and imaginative books being written in education today. Grounded on the theoretical advances in criticalism, feminism, and postmodernism in the last two decades of the twentieth century, Counterpoints engages the meaning of these innovations in various forms of educational expression. Committed to the proposition that theoretical literature should be accessible to a variety of audiences, the series insists that its authors avoid esoteric and jargonistic languages that transform educational scholarship into an elite discourse for the initiated. Scholarly work matters only to the degree it affects consciousness and practice at multiple sites. Counterpoints' editorial policy is based on these principles and the ability of scholars to break new ground, to open new conversations, to go where educators have never gone before.

For additional information about this series or for the submission of manuscripts, please contact:

Joe L. Kincheloe & Shirley R. Steinberg
c/o Peter Lang Publishing, Inc.
29 Broadway, 18th floor
New York, New York 10006

To order other books in this series, please contact our Customer Service Department:
(800) 770-LANG (within the U.S.)
(212) 647-7706 (outside the U.S.)
(212) 647-7707 FAX

Or browse online by series:
www.peterlang.com